VOLCANO

For my son

for Montserratians living in exile

for those living with her

and for those who loved me
so that i could start again.

VOLCANO

YVONNE MARY SELINA WEEKES

PEEPAL TREE

First published in Great Britain in 2006,
reprinted 2011, 2024

Peepal Tree Press Ltd
17 King's Avenue
Leeds LS6 1QS
UK

© Yvonne Mary Selina Weekes
Preface © Kamau Brathwaite Introduction
© Howard Fergus

All rights reserved
No part of this publication may be
reproduced or transmitted in any form
without permission

ISBN 9781845230371

CONTENTS

Kamau Brathwaite: Preface   7

Howard Fergus: Introduction   9

Chapter 1:   Soufriere   15

Chapter 2:   My First Relocation   32

Chapter 3:   'God Will Find a Way'   50

Chapter 4:   My Study Leave   65

Chapter 5:   Can you see my Country Burning?   80

Chapter 6:   The Evergreen Tree   87

Chapter 7:   Rising from the Ashes   108

PREFACE

The beauty of the Caribbean is (re)born out of the
catastrophic origins of the Yucatan-Atlantis cordillera
and the volcanoes & earthQuake flues
& flows that rim & ruim the Caribbean Sea - the eyes
& ears of epic memory for those of us that have songs
to see and geopsychic hearts to hear -
Port Royal 1692. Pelée/St Pierre 1902. the Soufriere
Hills of Montserrat since July 1995

The stories from Port Royal are now almost mythical
- a whole 'city of sin' under water; and no one has yet
spoken from the ashes of St Pierre . but in the *Volcano*
of Yvonne Selina Weekes we have at last the word
emotions of a daughter of the millennium mountain
& impediment itself. someone who feel it breathe: the
signal plume. the ash. the spume. the sulphur bleak &
blast. the detonations of the heart to heart. the
mountain blossom that will destroy the island's bloom
- 'a desart whiteness to the sea and on the sea' and
finally the fire. tears. the tears of the memory of that
original annunciation that tear even her body from
her native land. but nvr the soul. nvr the language of
indomitable possession repossession. eQual even to
the volcano taking over and counter-imaged in the
eQual ancient Evergreen - the tree of life round
which her humain poem turns and even burns

This is for us a moment of great fortune. That one of
us is privileged to testimony see into the chaotic crisis
heart of the beginning of the Caribbean and return to
tell the tale.

Kamau Brathwaite

INTRODUCTION

Almost every Montserratian who has experienced the long and direful night of the 1995 volcanic eruption has a story to tell. The facts, tone and colouring may differ but all will gush forth with strong emotion. A gifted creative writer and dramatist, Yvonne Weekes is well positioned to produce a spirited account which, while personal to her, is also personal to others of us. Hers is a private voice with universal resonance. This is a strength of the piece.

Volcano is not conventional memoir; it is a diary of events, imaginative narration, poetry, philosophising and editorialisation withal. This creative and coherent potpourri of lived experience and reflection is always interesting and most times engrossing. The memoir illustrates the centrality of the burning mountain to a sensitive soul and a hapless people.

The manifold effects of the crisis are dramatically portrayed: the ubiquitous ash, the shifting verities of the scientists, shelter life with toilets overflowing, death of plants, death of laughter, the resurrection of tension over UK racism mixed with seemingly white domination at home and death to love-making. Weekes found this last easier in Barbados, though sometimes all so fleeting and often not satisfying. One is tempted to identify her with the woman in one of her poems (in the volume) to whom men at times offer

> no more than a limp penile gesture
> which she laughs at

mocking them and ironically mocking the woman too, with 'love' so hollow, as described in lines so full of sadness and pathos. There is even a volcanic assault on discriminating taste as one rastaman perceives it: 'Me no eat tin food and dem tings there'.

Although it created a physical and psychological wasteland, "the mountain is my muse", the author asserts, inspiring prose and poetry, some of it of therapeutic value. "Writing helps – I write about how I feel". There is an ambivalence, though, in the way the mountain is regarded. While it inspires, it fragments and she understandably responds to it with both fear and fascination, as do we all for varying reasons.

Volcano is no detached narrative. The people in the pages come alive and are relatives and friends, son and lovers, and the mountain spilling its innards and muddying its sides is an external reflection of the author's inner reality and reaction to her 'refugee' experience; for "a deep black mud is covering up all my life's bricks. All my lavender dreams are on fire. I am more bereft than ever." Beautiful but sad.

In a similar vein, there is an alluring honesty in the author's treatment of her experience. She is transparent on failed relationships and does not scruple to offer intimate glimpses of her own love-making. There is honesty also about her wavering religious faith in the face of a natural mayhem and supposedly divine indifference, and generally she is not ashamed of the soft underbelly of religion. "So I sit down on the floor, on my bed, on the toilet, wherever, and just ask God to provide all my needs." Weekes is for real, credible, and the reader is on her side.

Weekes introduces a different tone when she editorialises. She speaks with authority on the mismanagement of the volcanic crisis. She lampoons indiscriminately, exposing the sins of managers for all the world to see like little boys who have not yet graduated to trousers. But prudence and honesty soon set in and she unashamedly admits after her management thesis: "I know the answers are more complicated." And one nods, "Amen."

It should not be surprising that this introspective gut-spilling artist gets philosophical in seasons of fear. "It can really motivate and propel a person into action…" she avers. "In that terrible blackness, that blackness of mortality, that blackness which clutches at me I begin to think about Jesus." Blackness is symbolic and the author is just saved from using it in a stereotypical fashion by the fact that the volcano does in reality produce many a black hour even at high noon. Intriguingly, Weekes alludes to an Evergreen tree in Plymouth where she with others laughed and 'limed'. Downed but not out, it symbolises, for her, permanence and an abiding sense of home. She may well find to her chagrin that the volcano is no respecter of landmarks and under its fiery sway all things become movable.

By definition, *Volcano* is no novel and the author has no obligation to sharply depict characters. There are, however, interesting glimpses through broad strokes of her pen. The chief persona, she reveals much of herself – hopes, fears, psychic burden and yes, the people she loves and loathes at her worst moments. You get some sense of the personality of persons close to her such as a grandmother and her stories within the story and her son Nathan who has inherited the creative gene causing him to craft phrases too big for boys like a "supernatural darkness".

A successful memoir of this imaginative sort cannot be divorced from the devices which portray it. The author writes in the present tense, which suggests immediacy, intimacy, listener/reader friendliness, a conversational tone and all those positive clichés. Her occasional graphic descriptions appear like golden nuggets gleaming on the pages. My favourite is linked to the superstitious white-of-egg oracle of folklore with its unique imagery: "There are thin red streaks, like veins in a blood-shot eye running through and through"; and there are lilting prose passages pulsing under the poet's hand like the one on bread. "Bread and hope. Bread and safety" etc., with its functional repetition helping to ensure that the emotional effect is richly earned.

I have always known the author as a talker, to employ a euphemism. In V*olcano* that penchant is artistically harnessed in the painting of scenes, volcanic and otherwise, in performance poetry and in her role as raconteur worthy of a worldwide audience. *Volcano* is a worthy prose take-off for a creative writer of rare talent with rarified heights to soar. She has heaved real life onto the stage and onto the pages of her memoir in an arresting and fascinating fashion.

> Howard A. Fergus KBE PhD
> Professor of Eastern Caribbean Studies (retired)
> University of the West Indies
> 10 August 2006

VOLCANO

CHAPTER 1

Soufriere

Soufriere: the mountain, the dormant dominant volcano, a sleeping giant. In all the years growing up and living on the island of Montserrat, I never once remember thinking about her. I don't remember what she looked like. I don't remember even noticing her. She was simply there. I only know that she came into my consciousness when she first blew that hot July in 1995. Before that day, she was never there for me.

This then is the beginning of *time*.

But not so for the villagers who live in the South and East. For years they live and work on her. They recognise her every curve and bend. They walk through her lush crevices and fertile gullies. They smell her dark fragrances. They cross her deep ravines to plant their food and tie their animals. They recall her secrets as told to them by their grandparents. One day they look up at her and they know something is wrong. They know even before the scientists who come to explore and examine her. They feel her intermittent shaking that whole year. They hear her loud rumbling and her persistent cries. These sounds are new to them. When one afternoon she finally coughs up her belly with hot steam and deadly gases, it is no surprise to them.

When I first hear the news about the volcano I am not at home. I am in Trinidad attending a conference on the role that non-Government agencies can play in sustainable development for the Caribbean region. I hear it. And the information floats right over me. I try to imagine what is actually happening. Or which mountain they are talking about. Naturally, I am anxious to return home. Montserrat is in the news and I want to be there.

On the flight I think about 'home'. Strange word. Home. Actually, I was born in a cold wintry London and the first time I hear the word Montserrat is when my parents decided to return 'home'. 1967. I go to school and tell my white English teacher that I am leaving to go to' Montserrat'. In front of a sea of white children she says; "There is no such place." And triumphantly brings out a globe to prove it. And amidst laughter and the tears welling in my throat, I see indeed "there is no such place!"

Despite this teacher, my family and I arrive in Montserrat, where the sun rises above breathtaking, blue mountains. I know a lot of people have never heard of Montserrat. Once I saw a tourist wearing a T-shirt in Montserrat that said: "Where the hell is Montserrat?" I even think about writing a book called: *Where the hell is Montserrat?* But then I figure since so few people have heard of Montserrat, why would they even look at a book with that title?

You would have to know something about this place that I call home. Montserrat has always been the world's best-kept secret. At one point in our history George Martin discovers her (we are always being discovered and then forgotten), builds a recording studio, 'Air Studios', and many famous artistes come by to record their music. Nobody notices them. They all bring big, burly bodyguards and promptly send them back.

In Montserrat I can leave my house open and come back to find everything just as I left it. Montserrat is what you might call a slow, meandering island where everybody limes and everyone is related. Like a royal family.

Before the volcano, Montserrat is just a tiny island, 39.6 square miles, which is run by, (and still is run by) a white British Governor. It has a population so small that it is actually the only island in the Caribbean that has a population growth below zero. I read that somewhere. Its other claim to fame is that it has the smallest museum in the world. I read that somewhere, too.

Now if you ask me why I say Montserrat is 39.6 square miles, the truth is I really am not sure how big she is supposed to be. When I went to school I learnt that Montserrat is a "tiny island completely surrounded by sea and is situated in the archipelago called the Caribbean with Guadeloupe to the south-east and Antigua to the north-east. It **is** only 32 square miles and has three mountain ranges." I learn this parrot fashion. So it is indelibly marked in my brain. Later, someone starts saying 39.6. You cannot forget the point six. Because it makes us bigger than Nevis, I think. So I guess Montserrat just grew. Like a child does in the summer. Except that nobody notices because the child has been around you all the time. But your relatives from overseas do. *You* only realize because his school pants are too short when he tries them on the first day of school. At any rate since this volcano, Montserrat has definitely grown!

I spend six years in "the place that does not exist" and then return to England in the summer of 1973 in order to get "a good British education". My father's words and my mother's notion. Not a single girl I meet at school or anyone at University has ever heard of Montserrat. Not even the black students.

In fact, the first night I spend in the hall of a teacher's training college in Kent, I am busy unpacking when a white student knocks on my door.

"Where do you come from?"

"London," I tell her. She seems friendly.

"No, I mean, where do you really come from?"

She says the word *really* with her bright red head of hair tilted. She seems to me like a Cocker Spaniel. So I tell her, "Montserrat."

"Oh," she responds. "Is that where they swing from tree to tree like monkeys?"

Honestly. I do not reply. For me, Montserrat with its deep black sands glittering as if diamonds were embedded in them, with its brilliant waters and saw-toothed mountains is home. It will always be home. England, then, is just a blur and really, once back home again in 1987, there is never any place on this earth where I would rather be. So I'll just skip all that England stuff – the England memories – just refer to it as 'the dry period'.

The first thing I remember being taught when I arrive

at school – between the good old Montserratian licks which the teachers meted out daily, whether you were good or bad, bright or dunce as a bat (my head teacher's words not mine) – is that Montserrat is a volcanic island. And that the volcano is dormant. This doesn't mean one earthly thing to me at the time, or even for a long time after that. The only thing it means is that there is a Soufriere which we teenagers visit during the school holidays and which stinks of rotten eggs. And little wisps of steam can be seen coming out of the yellow mustard rock. And the steam is boiling hot and can really burn you if your foot slips into the sticky soil. There is a hot water pond near the Montserrat Springs Hotel that is way past the town, and the water bubbles all the time because there is a vein in it from Soufriere. I don't quite know how that works, but I go in the water for a good soak. And after all that, I still remain oblivious to the mountain.

Once my friend Patsy and I went up to the top of Chances Peak where the major dome is situated. Being completely out of shape, the walk nearly kills me. This is in 1994, before the earth starts rumbling. We walk all two thousand, two hundred and thirteen steps to the top. Did I count all the steps? Well, yes, I really did. The view is breathtaking and I can see the whole island on a cloudless day. I also take my son and all my friends who visit Montserrat from time to time to the Great Alps Waterfall that is on the other side of the Soufriere, where the water is cool and exhilarating and takes my breath away. Still the idea of the mountain itself remains vague, in a mist.

Of course that is then. Now there is nothing left of

the waterfall so I am thankful that I visited all of her beauties before they vanished, because that's how Montserrat used to be. No one can do or see any of these things ever again. Because after three hundred years of deep slumber, the Langs Soufriere has roared into life and nobody can understand why.

When I arrive home from that conference, the airport is in chaos with many people trying desperately to leave, people trying to get on a flight to Antigua, the nearest island. The plane holds only fifty-four seats and people are literally climbing over the counters while immigration officers are asking them to be patient. They are terrified. There is panic. Montserrat is abuzz with activity. Scientists from all over the world come to visit; speculate about all the likely volcanic scenarios; discuss whether there is the likelihood of a full-scale volcanic eruption. The first sign of ash sends people scurrying. Some sanctimonious individuals of the hellfire and damnation persuasion are on the radio reminding us of our terrible sins. They see the volcano as God's way of punishing us for all the evils that we have committed as a people and reminding us of the need to repent. But quite frankly I can't imagine us as being more wicked than the people of, say, another small island which we all know has gone to the 'birds'. Others of a somewhat different religious hue want the people to pray and have faith in God's infinite kindness, since He will never destroy the people of Montserrat and prayer will solve everything. I wonder if they have heard of the flood or of Sodom and Gomorrah.

I was definitely not going anywhere. And frankly most people didn't believe that anything was going to happen. EVER! For me this is history in the making. Something I will be able to share with my grandchildren, whenever I get some. An old geography teacher tells me that he couldn't have wished to be born at a better time. This is a period of great historical and geological significance. Even though I am quite useless at both history and geography I readily agree with him. I mean, how many people actually get to see God creating a mountain? How many will ever see the steam like a billion pots of boiling water blowing from His nostrils? Flames flowing from His mouth and rolling down the mountain? His feet stamping all over the ground and shaking everything, reshaping the land, as if it is nothing at all. It is like a Hollywood movie. Moses parting the sea in *The Ten Commandments*. Or was it Charlton Heston? Only this is better. It is not a Hollywood special effect. I am here. I can actually see the new land that God is creating whenever I fly home on LIAT. I see the mountain turning inside out. I see the mountain growing before my eyes. I actually see the day turn into night in a moment. I am part of a history bigger and greater than the ten thousand people who live on the island and who have to bend to His will.

I become fascinated with the mountain. She looks beautiful and majestic. She looks bigger, enthralling. I realize how little I really know about her. I do not know her like the people of the South and the East. So I start visiting her. And it seems everyone else on the island has the same idea. People walk up to the Tar River House. It is an old plantation house and they park their cars in droves and walk along the Tar River, cameras in hand, to see the mountain. It is like a pilgrimage with people standing and watching in awe as she puffs great columns of steam from deep within her belly. She seems to pull us to her. There is thick silvery water running from the mountain like mercury. I try never to turn my back on her.

Even from a distance we watch her. We watch her by day and by night. We watch her as we are driving from the North and as we are driving to the North. On our single stretch of smooth road, where drivers drive at breakneck speed, we slow down to watch the mountain. We watch the mountain while we gossip and when we go for our early morning jog. We watch her while we drink and eat at the Harbour Court, a restaurant owned by my good friend Mr. Watts, where we meet every Friday to discuss the serious issues of the day and to pass judgment. I suspect that we probably watch the mountain in our sleep too. I can personally testify to the fact that I slept with one eye open for at least six months. There is almost no conversation in which the mountain does not feature.

We listen constantly to the daily and nightly volcano reports. In these early days, the radio is on all twenty-four hours, with the manager seeming to single-handedly 'woman' the station. I realize quite early that there are going to be some individuals who will be picked out for some kind of Queen's award or other. I really do sleep with one eye open in case anything should happen in the night. The smell of sulphur creeps up the ghaut behind my house and into my bedroom. It reminds me of ghosts and makes me shiver.

But most of all, people talk to one another. There are passionate and angry discussions outside rum shops and under the Evergreen Tree between mothers and daughters, sons and fathers, husbands and wives, friends and enemies about whether the volcano will blow or not, but ....

"Not a ting a happen."

"The scientists no know wha dem a say."

"Gal, de mountain a grow. You can't see?"

Everyone has become an expert in volcanology and seismology. The Evergreen Tree in the heart of Plymouth is the centre of all activity. When Hugo, that dreadful hurricane, came in 1989, he tried to blow her down but she was not to be beaten. She has been with us for over three hundred and fifty years listening to our stories, shading our bodies from the sun with her huge fronds, providing shelter from the rains. She can turn into a makeshift venue for midday barbecues; a place for teenage lovers to hide from parents or a refuge for a struggling drunk. The Evergreen tree is everything to us. And the fiercest arguments about the volcano obviously take place there.

There are scientists from all over the globe. Some seem to be serious about their task. Others seem to be having a whale of a time drinking and partying at Andy's bar, which is not too far away from the Volcano Observatory. Dr. Ambeh, the head scientist, has an excitement about the volcano that can be contagious. I remember the first time I met him. I had taken Carol Lawes, the Cultural Officer for CARICOM, on a fact-finding mission around the island that day. (CARICOM is a regional organization set up by politicians to create integration in the Caribbean. At every party I go to where there are Caribbean people present, I figure we should invite the politicians, so we can show them Caribbean integration – party style.) Ambeh makes the whole study of volcanoes and earthquakes seem so accessible for us that, as a result of that visit, I arrange for groups of children from the primary schools to visit the observatory and, hopefully, demystify the entire experience for them.

I notice that all kinds of officials of various shades arrive and there are secret and seemingly high-level discussions about which people are very suspicious. I say secret because whenever I am visiting a particular hotel, having a drink with friends or something, I notice that the Governor and a set of White scientists are sitting huddled together. Even though the volcano is being monitored by the Seismic Research Centre, which is based in Trinidad, no scientist with my complexion is ever there. I am not the only one who notices these discussions. So soon the Evergreen is buzzing with news of racism in the Volcano Observatory. It finally comes out in the newspapers months later and the Governor announces that there is no basis whatsoever for such allegations, but he is going to get to the bottom of it. We laugh because it is stale news to us.

The most important of the discussions under the Evergreen centre around which parts of the island are safe and which parts are not. I feel pretty safe where I live, in the village of Corkhill. At least that's what I tell everyone. But secretly I believe that one night we will all be told to get up and run. Except that there will be nowhere to run to. And it will be too late anyway. It is now August 1995. The early days. Not much is happening. New vents open up here and there. Of course, there remains a little tingle of excitement since Montserrat is now continually in the regional and international news. We feel a kind of fear mixed with fascination that few people will admit.

Then on 7th August 1995, the scientists announce that the people of Long Ground and Farms, villages furthest to the east, will have to move into shelters. These are basically the churches and schools in the north of the island. People become really nervous. I am thinking now, *Please let's not panic. This whole thing is going to blow over in a month*. I never for a moment think the mountain is going to stop me from fulfilling my dreams and my goals. But the mountain? Well, she seems to have other plans.

On 12 August, we have a whole set of earthquakes so bad and so frightening that the whole house starts trembling, my whole dressing table arrangement gets messed up, the television starts shaking, my books come tumbling down. I begin to wonder what I will do if I'm in the house alone and suddenly the walls start to cave in, as I had seen on those television newscasts of earthquakes in Mexico and Nicaragua. I have no idea what to do. No one has told us anything about what to do when an earthquake comes. Hurricanes: yes. Earthquakes: no.

By the middle of August, I am busy preparing to go to Trinidad for CARIFESTA VI. It is the premier regional celebration of culture and the arts. The Minister of Education and Culture insists we take a school choir and it is decided that we will take the children who have just won the island's Schools Arts Festival. They are an excellent choir and despite the fact that this means a whole heap of extra work for me, I, like the students, teachers and parents of the Bethel School, am excited. The trouble is that in the middle of preparing the choir, these are the very children who have to move from their villages. They are scattered all over the place and I suddenly have my workload doubled.

It is while we are at CARIFESTA that things turn worse at home. Naturally, most of us spend our money calling home. Although we all wanted to be at CARIFESTA, our thoughts are undoubtedly at home with our families. It is sometimes difficult to focus on the business of preparing for performances. Everyone is preoccupied and anxious. On top of this, we are the centre of much attention. The media follow me around. They turn up at rehearsals. They are outside my room when I wake up in the morning. When I'm at the CARIFESTA village, they appear outside the booth where we have Montserrat items on display. Even when I am out enjoying the performances of other countries, some media person is suddenly in my face with a camera and microphone. They become entirely obtrusive and irritate me.

We get the news on Wednesday morning at five o'clock on the 23rd August that the entire population has to move north of the Belham River, that is, to move to the north of the island. My heart becomes almost anaesthetised. I call my cousin Laureen at home and, of course, when she doesn't answer the phone I almost have a nervous breakdown. Everyone is fraught with anxiety, worried about the loved ones they have left at home. We try to keep it quiet from the children whose parents have already been relocated, but they soon realize something is amiss. The question that troubles us most: what will happen to the children and us if there is really an explosion that prevents us from returning to Montserrat? The fact that we are responsible for these children weighs heavily on the six adults in the group. We meet at six that morning and pray together in hushed tones for God to save our island. Everyone is crying. I think my colleague Myrle's body will break, and anyone who knows her will understand that this would be quite something, as Myrle is one big woman. Big, and beautiful!

On top of all this, we have to perform the play *Women + Men +Women*, at the Little Carib Theatre in Port of Spain, Trinidad. And what with going to bed at 2 a.m. after liming with Myrle and Hodge that night, and being hounded by the press that entire day, I am pretty exhausted by the time the lights go down for the show. We get a standing ovation. I think we are brilliant too, but partly it's because no one had expected us to perform with the volcano threatening to destroy everything and everyone we love. So I feel that the standing ovation is for our courage and strength, too. And because the people simply love us. I don't think I have ever cried so much at the end of a performance. There are a lot of Barbadians in the audience, including Cynthia Wilson and Andrew Pilgrim, some of that country's stalwarts in theatre. Is it a sign?

I cannot go home. My village has been relocated and my son is already in England, so I decide that's where I should go for the holidays that I have coming. Besides, I haven't been to England for eight years, so my family decides that it is high time for me to pay them a visit. I acquiesce. I don't enjoy being there. Sure, I have missed my sisters and their children. But my whole heart and mind are in Montserrat. I can't sleep. I keep imagining the worst. To top it all, my entire family fully expects me to stay in England. They just can't understand that Montserrat is my home and no way am I planning to leave there.

Added to all this grief, while I sit in England not particularly enjoying the weather, two hurricanes pass by Montserrat: Luis and Marilyn. I watch the news on BBC television and hold my breath for at least five minutes. On television, there are people I know waiting for the volcano to blow and the dreaded hurricanes to pass over the St Maarten de Porres Catholic Church, which I attended. They are cramped and look downright uncomfortable. I swear that God must really have it in for us in truth. But thankfully, the island is spared and I return. One of my neighbours tells me that she was staying in a tent and that the high winds blew it down and everyone got soaked. So I am grateful that I didn't have to go through that.

While in England, I hear that our Chief Minister is threatening civil servants with dismissal if they don't return to the island by a certain date. One of my aunts, who lives in Florida, hears this too and blows a gasket, sending a message to me to go back to Montserrat or I might lose my job. I find her reaction quite remarkable since this is the same aunt who got absolutely hysterical the week the volcano first blew. She had been phoning me the whole week and when she got no response, her imagination rioted. People are strange creatures.

I just think that the ash must have got into the Chief Minister's brain, because people are genuinely frightened of this volcano and his attitude clearly sucks. I think he'd better start showing a little respect to the mountain.

I take my sweet time to go back home since I'm in no hurry to leave my son. I have already decided, reluctantly, that it is best for him to remain in England at this time, especially as the volcano has everyone, except perhaps the Chief Minister, nervous. This decision, on reflection, has less to do with what everyone else thinks is best for my son and more to do with my feelings of powerlessness and helplessness since clearly good old Langs Soufriere is in control. I am not.

I leave my son in England with his father. At the airport he clings onto me for dear life. The parting is extremely distressing. The feeling is worse when I get home; I miss him so much that I simply want him there with me. By now I am getting used to living with the volcano and it doesn't really affect my village that much. Besides, being back home, I am much more relaxed and soon begin to realize that the British press has made the whole thing much more frightening than it actually is. So, after much thinking, I decide that volcano or not, my son is much better off with me. Besides, my telephone bill to England is so astronomical I might as well buy him a ticket. That's another thing. Cable and Wireless is sure making a lot of money out of us. Everyone I know is perpetually calling his or her family in London, New York, wherever, just to keep them up to date as to what is happening at home, and to check up on those they have sent abroad.

I now blame the press for a lot of the garbage that

is being said about Montserrat. My relatives and friends overseas have a hard time dealing with the news accounts that reach them. My mother declares that she will never step foot on Montserrat again after seeing the BBC coverage. My sisters think I am mad for wanting to remain on the island after hearing some of the stories. They can't understand why my cousin Laureen and I are not returning to England. Many of my friends from overseas call regularly. They want to know what support they can offer me, personally, and to find out what they can send to help the people of the island. The press makes it seem as if we are being blown away, so they are extremely anxious. Having been in England during the first relocation and seeing pictures of the mountain – and this before the mountain really began to do its thing – I know exactly how they feel. Terrified.

Of course, nothing much has changed since then. The press still shows Montserrat burning down to the ground. They still show the squalor of the shelters. They show the huge ash plumes going sometimes thirty thousand feet in the air. A good news item is when it closes down the airport in Columbia, which it actually does, throwing air traffic into total confusion. Or when the ash covers St. Vincent. Now *that* gets them in a scare about their own Soufriere. The choicest news item is the threat of a tidal wave that will cover all the low-lying land of Barbados. This is good headline stuff. Later I imagined the irony of being washed away by a tidal wave as a result of the volcano, after having moved to Barbados to get away from it. They still talk about how resilient and spirited we are as a people. All good stuff for selling newspapers. The Press is in cahoots with the British Government, systematically putting out information which is misleading and false. It is the most efficient way of dispossessing us.

One day, my mother writes and sends her bankbook. She believes that the reason I remain is obvious. I don't have the money or else I would certainly leave Montserrat. The fact is I will remain put. She, of course, does not understand. She asks me if I want to kill her grandson. She informs me that God has turned His back on Montserrat because the 'people dem too bad'. She tells me that God has given us a warning and who can't hear will surely feel, so I ought to leave immediately. I don't respond to her letter. I make my own decisions. I'm impervious.

I decide it is time for my son to come home. I call him one day and he tells me that the school is awful. The other students in his class are rude and give the teacher a hard time; she is soft and cries and he feels bad because the children who behave the worst are black and the work is boring and too easy and he finishes all the work in no time at all. I call back that evening and tell his father to send my child home immediately. No discussion.

As it turns out, I believe that I have made the right decision because when my son Nathan arrives he tells me that he was so worried about me dying in the volcano that he used to hide in his room and cry at night. He is happy to be home. My family and his father's family, on the other hand, are not exactly over the moon. I think that they have their troubles. I have mine. The mountain – well she has her own her thing to do.

CHAPTER 2

My First Relocation

The day my son arrives home from England is the same day of the island's second relocation and my first at work. My village still does not have to move and I am grateful for that. But my son's paternal family in England try to give me a hard time although I really don't take them on. We all have our lives to live. I don't believe the volcano is going to take my life or anyone else's for that matter. Provided we listen to the scientists. But if we have to go I want my son with me.

December 1995, the first of my own personal trials begins. Our offices are now at the Salem Secondary School where, also, over two hundred people are living. When I go to work in the morning there are mothers bathing their children at an outside tap; men sitting around staring aimlessly into space; clothes flapping above our heads; the squeals of children playing. The Public Works Department has its huge vehicles across the way and their engines are kicking up a storm. The upper half of the Secondary School has lessons and there is general pandemonium as the entire Secondary School staff of sixty share the same small staff room amidst chairs and desks piled up to make room for the 'shelterees'.

The weekend of our second relocation I have to put on my thinking cap. Because of the heavy ash falls and the rise in volcanic activity, schools closing early and operating as shelters. How on earth am I going to continue work as Director of Culture? I am convinced that culture will be the last thing on people's minds. Particularly the administrators. They will only be concerned with distributing beds, masks and food rations, and issuing orders. So I come up with an idea, run it by a few of my friends and present it to the Minister on Monday morning.

By this time there are twenty-six shelters, ranging from churches to schools. Teachers, as usual, are getting blows in the press – what's new? As if it is their fault that they are home doing nothing. I come up with a way of using a small group of teachers – twelve to be exact – to run a programme of cultural activities. This includes storytelling, drama, music – singing and dancing – and art and craft. I am given some money to hire some really talented artists who would otherwise have been sitting home unable to work. It is a rough programme but hugely rewarding. Some shelters, like those in the village of Salem where the majority of children are relocated, are simply overwhelming. One day we have over two hundred children singing and swinging away down the road following their teachers. It is a truly wonderful sight. Even though the programme is just for those children who are in shelters, everyone brings their children. It is a huge hit with everyone. We are overworked, but I am glad to be out of the office. The children sit on my lap and I play mother. Or Santa Claus. Gifts from businesses and private individuals start to pour in. Everyone is happy to give, and on the last day of the programme and two tired weeks later we are able to give many gifts to the children. We all go away with a huge headache. But one thing is certain, according to one shelter manager, the children, who before were restless and found it difficult to settle down at night, are now too tired for anything after the day's activities. Not even the mountain could stop us from giving to the children a much-needed respite. Mission accomplished.

By 2nd January 1996, most people are back in their homes and offices and life seems to go back to normal. The people of Long Ground go home a month later. The mountain still puffs and blows. Light ash falls in Dagenham and Amersham but people are by now getting used to watching and living with the mountain. Most people are more preoccupied with living.

On the first day of work after the holidays, my boss comes in and says he has a big favour to ask of me. I have already seen it coming and am prepared for this. One of the teachers has left the Ministry of Education and the Secondary School is in a pickle. The students, who have exams to take in June, have no teacher. The teacher in question had already warned me. He was one of the people on Montserrat preaching gloom and doom. He thought the island was heading for disaster, that the volcano was dangerous and that people were mad to want to remain there. He admonished me hundreds of times.

"Oh, Yvonne Weekes, no take no chance with your son. You have to leave this island!" He was terrified. I thought at that time he was being melodramatic and needed to calm down. Anyway he left. And I get lumbered. Some of us cannot say no.

So now, armed with two jobs and the mountain, life goes on as though normal. Nobody really gives much thought to the fact that the mountain is still puffing and blowing. I try, like most other people, not to let her interfere with the really important occasions like Valentine's Day or St Patrick's Day or the Easter Monday fete at the beach.

I do something strange this Easter. I remember that when I was about twelve my maternal grandmother came to visit us from London. Mama. When she arrived she was this short, really black woman. So black that she seemed almost featureless. She was frightening because the left side of her face was twisted as the result of a stroke. But she told me all kinds of stories about the old days. It was Easter day when she told me that if I cracked the white of an egg and put it in a glass of water and then looked at it in the midday sun, I would see the face of my future husband. For years I used to do this and never once did I see anything like *any* lover. During the dry spell of my life – the England spell – I forgot all about this superstitious nonsense. But this Easter I decide to try it. Out of pure nostalgia for my childhood. The truth is I'm not interested in seeing *any* man's face, because if I did see a face, I'm sure I'd jump right out of my skin.

But this Easter I decide to try it. I hide the egg so that my son does not see it. I would not know how to deal with his question. At midday I go to see what the future holds for me. And what do I see? The egg is like fire. There are these thin red streaks, like veins in a bloodshot eye, running through. And I swear I can see the mountain in the glass as clear as if I am standing in the yard hanging out my clothes. I feel the hairs on the back of my neck stand up and I dash the glass and its contents down into the ghaut behind the house. My heart is racing and pounding because I realise that the mountain is going to dictate my future.

It is just around that time the scientists stop everyone from visiting the mountain. Of course, people still go. By then the catch phrase is:

Scientists are still viewing the mountain with grave concern.

But somehow, some of us still do not really believe that the mountain is dangerous. At night there is an incandescent glow, as if God is fanning the dying embers of His huge coal pot.

People drive up to strategic points, like the back road to the airport from the north of the island, and cool out in their cars under the stars just to see the mountain's fire. Well, they do other things too. Like making passionate love. Once a friend and I go to see the glow together. Cars are lined up as far as the eye can see. Some are moving up and down in rhythm and the windows are thoroughly steamed up. We just drive away as quietly as we can. I don't want to try to see who is doing what with whom. At least that is one way of ensuring some privacy. Probably uncomfortable though.

After March 17 it starts ashing heavily in town. Plymouth begins to look as if it has been caught in a desert storm. My mind goes back to those pictures on CNN during the American Gulf War in Iraq. We have to wear masks to work. These masks are issued by the Emergency Operation Centre. Frankly, they are a waste of time. Now, the plush Government Headquarters (which the British Government never did quite manage to hand over to the local government) is covered in ash. With their air-conditioned offices, the water fountain and carpeted offices (some!) – and the ash, of course, we have worked there for only eight months. By 3rd April 1996 we have to move. Never to return.

What is so interesting about this time is that, for the first time since the volcano started doing its thing, my cousin Laureen and I decide we're going to a meeting to hear what the scientists have to say. This is on 2nd April 1996. The day before there was a huge pyroclastic flow at Tar River and Long Ground, which has everyone thinking about that word: Relocation. The volcano sends up columns of ash so high that there is ash everywhere. The Government sets up meetings so that the people can talk directly to the scientists, to the members of the Health Service and to them. Although I have pretty much made up my mind that I don't want to hear anything the government has to say – I mean who does? – we brave the ash and go to the meeting at eight o'clock that night. It is in an amazing million-dollar church, which the Pentecostals built, probably for a lot more than a million dollars. It has plush carpets and soft cushioned velvet pews and it's real big. The last time I'd been there was for some person's funeral, whose I could not remember just then. It had been sparkling, brilliant and polished and now it is covered in ash. As I walk on the carpet, my feet sink into the ash and get covered white, and when I sit on the seat, little wisps of ash come floating up to my throat, making me cough.

As I sit down, I wonder about a joke that I recently heard a young man crack. He said that at least women wouldn't need hair-spray any more since the ash is like spritz and makes your hair stiff. I had just had my hair done that same day and now I'm sure it looks a mess. I wonder about the significance of having the meeting in a church. I decide then that God is in our midst, and I feel reassured when I hear them say that there is no crack in the mountain, that it is not about to collapse. There will be no major relocation of the island – except for the people of Long Ground who have already had to move; and there will be nebulisers and asthma medication at all the health clinics to cope with the rise in asthmatic attacks. All of this the scientists and the Chief Medical Officer (acting) and the politicians say. So we don't have to drive to the north where the hospital has been set up in the primary school.

"What I want to know," one lady asks at the meeting, "is bout de ash." She is getting really heated.

"All me flowers and me plants and me herbs in me garden dead. And gone black." Some people start to laugh. She continues.

"So what I want to know: if me plants dead, well my insides must be black too. Because me a breathe de same ash."

More people laugh. I really can't understand why people find it funny. She has a valid point. We have all been breathing the ash for quite some time. Maybe we are dead too.

But a scientist explains that the root of the plant is

still alive. The plants only appear to be dead. Clever. They continue to talk in some high-flown language about silicosis, and acid rain, and respiratory problems, and masks, and electronic distance meters, and seismographs and shortening of lines, and all kinds of language which I feel sure is designed to confuse the people and keep them in ignorance.

There is mention of a Wadge and Isaacs report. So it is real. But we leave the meeting having swallowed 'hook, line and sinker' every word those politicians and scientists say, even though we've been looking at the mountain for days and full well know that she looks deadly.

Next day I go to work feeling weary. Even from my house I can see the pyroclastic flows coming down the side of the mountain. Now, my son's school has closed down since it's in the heart of town and they are busy transferring it up to the north of the island. So I drive my son to St John's where my grandmother lives and where Laureen has a hairdressing salon. At least I know he's safe. Then I drive back to work in town. Plymouth has become Ash City. I do not like the look of the mountain as I drive. It has been blowing up ash all day.

That whole day at work, there is a rumour going around that a major relocation of the East, South and Central areas of the island is pending. Well everyone in Montserrat knows that *long grass carry news and soursop bush bring it back*, so of course everybody believes it. I believe it. I'm beginning to think that we love drama. Even though, throughout the day, I can still hear the Acting Governor's recorded message from the previous day, telling us that there has been no escalation of activity, everybody is in disbelief. Ready to move.

Later that day I go to pick up my son, who tells me that he has had a great day helping his Auntie Laureen in the shop. I have to wonder how much help that really is. We begin our drive back home, driving towards the mountain. For the first time, we see ash falling in the north. The safe zone. I have my radio on. I hear the voice of the Acting Governor. He is asking everyone to move immediately from the areas south of where Laureen and I live. I can't believe this. Laureen is in front driving her car and seems to be in trouble. Her windscreen wipers are not working; she cannot see a thing, she says, as she comes to a stop. The ash is coming down heavier. Her radio is not working so I tell her the news. "Gal you lie!" she says. Even though I am telling her, I cannot believe it myself. We are still in the safe zone. We can barely see either in front of us or behind us. Then the washer for my windscreen wiper runs out of water. When it pours it really pours. We are in the north of the island and ash is coming down. We are in the safe zone. We stop by a mechanic and Laureen leaves her car. It is clear the car has some sort of electrical problem. I jump out of my car trying to dodge and duck the ash that is falling more heavily. My mind is racing as I try to piece together the scientists' words from the previous night. A thin layer of ash covers me as I fill my windscreen washer with water. When I get back into the car we can hear the Acting Governor's voice on the radio still droning on. The car windows are up. We all begin to sweat. Nathan starts taking off his clothes. The ash begins to sweep into the car. I drive slowly because I can see nothing as the sweat beads across my temples.

My headlights are on full now. We pass cars, trucks and lorries attempting to speed through the swirling ash to the safe zone. Vehicles are piled up with people, suitcases, boxes, trunks and a few memories. There is such a commotion, I know we are more likely to have an accident in the safe zone. All the warnings for us to drive carefully are completely ignored. I have to admit I just want to get home and inside as quickly as possible. I look at the faces of people driving towards me. Some people are looking as if they have shrunk, as if they are dreaming. Others are obviously cussing and fretting. Drivers are impatient. Naturally.

"Jesus Lord!" my cousin exclaims. "Ain't dem people say last night a we na relocate. A what a go on?"

She expresses my feelings exactly. I look up to heaven. The ash is still pouring. By the time we get home, outside both our houses looks like fields of snow. The ash has followed us all the way to the safe zone. I stay by Laureen until late. There is safety in numbers. We listen to the radio. There is a lot of talk on the radio from scientists and government officials trying to explain this new situation. They remind us that the volcano is unpredictable and has now gone into a more dangerous phase. Somehow I get the feeling that they've all been caught with their pants down. Inside of me feels like cold water. At least we have the weekend to come to terms with this new situation. I drive home down the hill. I'm not living too far away from my cousin. I go to bed feeling more despondent than I have ever felt in my life.

Later on my son writes a story about this incident. He does more justice to the whole scenario than I probably do. And he writes a line that really makes me laugh. Laugh out loud so that everyone can hear me. He writes: "I don't know if I was more afraid of the volcano or of my mother's driving!"

The radio station is on all night. I listen to all the reports. Nervously, because now the scientists are saying that there is a crack in the mountain. I listen to my son breathing next to me. I am frightened about leaving him to sleep in his own room. That night, for the first time, I actually listen to the Governor carefully. I get up and find all my important documents. Our passports, birth certificates, my divorce papers. Just in case. I realize and acknowledge that I am truly afraid. Perhaps I have been in denial all this time.

Damn. Life had been so wonderful before. I can see all my dreams fading away. I don't want to sleep. I want to be wide-awake and alert. Just in case. But I feel my feet falling to sleep. I am thinking. It's been over a year since the volcano started acting up. Like a spoilt child. Or is it more like a really spiteful mother? Or really a vengeful god? My waist eventually joins my feet. And like magic the rest of me follows and I am only awakened by the phone ringing the next morning.

A friend calls to ask how it feels to be ash-bound and to give me the latest joke by the Chief Minister. I don't know him to be funny but I am prepared to listen.

"Girl, the Chief Minister went up in a helicopter last week with scientists. And you no hear de joke?"

"Well, if I'd heard the joke, then I would know it."

"It was on the radio."

Why doesn't she get to the point?

"One of the reporters asks him why he feels so confident about the scientists' review of the situation. Does he really believe that it is safe for people to remain on the island? And you know what he say?"

She starts to laugh. This joke better be good.

"He says he knows it is safe because he see one yellow butterfly."

She roars. I don't get it. But the Opposition Members of Parliament have a field day. It is the standing joke of the times.

A lot of people move into my village, which is suddenly very crowded. It has always been a silent and sleepy village, which only comes alive at the weekends. On Fridays, there is a sound system which plays at the rum shop close by. A group of men play slamming dominos on the corner of the road. Young boys play basketball on the court right next to me. I can smell the sweat of their laughing bodies when I walk by. There is always a lot of life and laughter and liming at weekends, which is a welcome change. But I love the quiet of the weekdays, where sometimes you can hear the soft singing of a neighbour. The silence usually lulls me to sleep. But all that is gone. These days, in fact, every day, the noise level is simply unbearable and frightening. The walls shake, not just from the earth tremors, but from Gemini Hi Fi too.

For the first time, too, there are many people whom I just do not recognize. When I walk through the village, I feel as if some of the debris of society has fallen here. I no longer feel safe. A group of young men walk around the place as if they are warriors. Their chests are all puffed up and they seem taller than the buildings. My grandmother tells me that they are just children smelling themselves. But they behave as if they own the village. One night, I hear gunshots ringing out. The next day I hear that a young man was shot and is in a critical condition. I blame the volcano. People are now cramped up for the first time in our history. There is a lot of tension. People are living like pigs. I feel claustrophobic.

The local primary school is now a shelter. There are a lot of problems over there. I visit often because someone I know is living there. There are not enough toilets to accommodate the people. The showers and the toilets are overflowing. There is no refrigeration. There is no privacy. The children are a nuisance for those who don't have children. Some people come in late at night and disturb the others. There are lots of petty squabbles. When you put people to live in a small space, without the basic necessities of ordinary living, there is bound to be frustration and trouble. The shelter manager, who is a calm and beautiful lady, is at her wits' end. She wants me to speak to the children about sharing the responsibility of keeping the shelter clean. All the children know me so there is some measure of respect. I try to help by speaking to the children about keeping the bathroom and kitchen clean. I make numerous calls to assist them. Finally someone comes to fix the problems. Except they can't fix the pain and frustration. I don't know how they can possibly manage. There are about fifty people there, who are living together for the first time in a building that is after all a school.

The adults complain to me that the children are very

rude. I think they are just bored. School has not yet been set up and God only knows how that will happen when it, as all the other schools in the safe zone, is being used as a shelter. I take books and crayons and games to the shelter that a colleague in St. Thomas has sent to me for distribution to the children. Everyday I pass the school on my way to work, I feel guilty because I am still comfortably in my own home.

There is a local rumour that says the village is not safe. There is a scientific report. Wadge and Isaacs. Although no one I know has actually seen it. This report apparently says that Corkhill is not safe. In fact, according to this report, we should all be north of the Belham River. I wonder if this report actually exists. Perhaps it is like all other reports, shelved away, gathering dust in some important person's office. If the village has to move, this will be disastrous for those people who have actually relocated here. For them in particular, the whole situation is incomprehensible.

I wonder how it was that the first time there was a relocation, the scientists asked our village to move. When I went to England, Corkhill was in the unsafe zone and now we are being told that we are perfectly safe. We speculate on this. I remember the Wadge and Isaacs report. I promise myself that somehow I must get my hands on it. I begin to be aware that the mountain is actually overlooking my house. Before, even though she was never out of my mind, I couldn't actually see her. But these days my son and I can see the pyroclastic flows coming down the side of the mountain. Our house is near a ghaut, and if you are at the back of the house you can see the mountains of Molyneaux and Lees, which is the East. So, for the first time, it dawns on me that two kilometres away from the mountain, as the cock flies, is actually close.

"Girl, the Government can't move Corkhill because they not got nowhere to put people. They are playing with people's lives."

This makes a whole heap of sense to me. Corkhill has people from all over the island who seem to have set up home permanently. Some people I know are now paying rent for homes here, *and* paying their mortgages for homes they cannot live in.

"Where is the Government going to put people if Corkhill has to move?" my friend continues. "Besides, the Chief Minister says there is no such thing as an unsafe zone. Only a designated unsafe zone."

"Does this mean that there is no such thing as a safe zone? Only a designated safe zone," I ask.

My friend does not know the answer to that. The scientists keep saying that volcanology is not an exact science.

"The scientists don't know one cricket thing," my cousin says. If that is so, then anything is possible. I figure, at the end of all this palaver, someone will be committed. I pray only that it will not be me. I think that we must all be mad. Mad to continue living with this mountain. Yet I still feel no desire to leave despite the protestations of my family overseas. My mother is angry with me and older sister frustrated by my decision.

A friend of mine who works at the National Trust comes across a story in an American newspaper about the volcano. The story is that the volcano was bound to roar to life since we had no business disturbing the Amerindian burial site at Trants Estate, just at the foot of the mountain. The way I hear it, the minute those American archeologists moved a skeleton from out of the ground, the god Vulcan got real mad and decided to teach us a lesson. The message: either we put back the skeleton or we pay the price. The skeleton is still in some museum some place, being tested to figure out Montserrat's prehistory. While Vulcan still rages.

I become so preoccupied with this story that one Saturday I ask my grandmother whether she thinks we should have a jumbie dance. Ever since I hear that a jumbie dance will reveal all the evil in the community, I am willing to call upon these Caribbean spirits, or any spirits, if they will help. She laughs at me.

"Jumbie dance is not for that," she says. "You have a jumbie dance when people sick, especially children."

"The country sick," I say. "The country is real sick."

After that she begins to tell me about the jumbie dances which she used to go to as a child. How they used to lay out the table with rice and cassava for the jumbies. How they used to dance for sometimes three or even four nights. How the dancers used to turn as the spirit came inside them and spoke through them. How a spirit could go inside anyone, even an innocent bystander. How people used to be afraid of jumbie dances, especially those people who had some dark secret to hide.

I figure that with the skeleton out of the ground, perhaps there is some truth to this theory about why the volcano is so mad. I start talking to some of the old people who know about jumbie dance. A lot of them are in the Catholic Church, too. But even though they tell me a thing or two, they all think I'm slightly mad. Tan Tan, my grand aunt, tells me, "Child, since electricity come, no more jumbie around."

I find an old man still living in Streatham who used to play the fife. Even though Streatham is in the unsafe zone, he refuses to move. I consider *this* quite mad.

"Nobody care about the old ways," he tells me. At this point I am more concerned about why he has chosen to stay in his house, entirely alone, under the shadow of the volcano. He is not frightened of the volcano. He would rather die in his own house.

"Life is not like before," he says. "And nobody going to knock me about in no shelter and treat me like a child."

"It is madness to stay in the area," I tell him.

"Let it be so," he says.

"But you'll get killed!"

"Then let it be so," he repeats. I forget all about the jumbie business.

The madness continues at work. All government offices are now in a building in the safe zone. With ash. The entire Ministry of Education is in a single room. Two of my colleagues and I decide to put our desks on the patio of the building which used to be some kind of guesthouse for the rich and famous. There is a lot of tension as people juggle for space. High and low now have to rub shoulders. I am secretly amused. It is interesting how people bristle when they no longer have their Great House, when the servants and the overseers now have to share the same quarters. There is no longer a master bedroom and it is a humbling experience for some. Me, I love it. Or at least, seeing as how we are doing another cultural programme in the schools, and seeing as how I'm trying to complete the students' examination syllabus, and seeing as how I am busy writing a play to take to the shelters, and seeing as how every time I pass one of the schools that is in a tent, someone wants me to do something for them, I really have no time for the tensions which exist in that room. I thank God that there are people out there who need me.

CHAPTER 3

'God Will Find A Way'

The period of April 1996 to August 1996 is the most difficult and trying period of my entire life. It is also the most creatively challenging and exciting. By this time Montserrat has gone through its third relocation. Everyone who lived to the south of me has been relocated to shelters or friends or private homes, depending on whether they have the money to pay the now exorbitant charges for rent. All of the people I have grown close to over the nine years since I returned home have been relocated. And for the first time ash falls on Corkhill like rain. It pounds down on us. It beats us into our houses. It creeps into the curtains. It steals into the bed. It settles on the toothbrushes. It spreads itself on the bedroom rugs. It strips the paint off the outside walls. It blows into our lungs. We are continually watching the pyroclastic flows coming down the mountain. We try to guess which way the wind will blow the ash. And invariably it falls on us. It is almost impossible to hang out ones clothes on the line.

It is also the first time in Montserrat that I get lost. I can't find anywhere. All the business places have relocated. I never bothered to familiarize myself with these areas. So the first time I try to find Suntex bakery to buy bread I get thoroughly lost and never bother again, thus depriving myself of my favourite bread. What's worse, I can't find the post office. I can't find the banks. I can't find the market. I'm in the middle of my life. And I don't like feeling lost.

On Mother's Day 1996, I am by my cousin Laureen in the village of Weekes when suddenly the sky becomes quite overcast and we think it is going to rain. Only it isn't rain. It is ash. The heaviest that we have personally experienced. It falls like bullets on the galvanize roof. I feel that it is better to die in my own house. I grab my son and jump in the car to head down the hill. Ash falls solidly for about ten minutes. Then just as suddenly as it has come, the sky is bright and sunny and all seems to be well with the world. Only everywhere is as white as snow. Dust swirls around just like a snowstorm. On the radio, the scientists are telling us not to go outside and insisting that everyone wear dust masks.

Both Patsy and Paulette call to find out how Nathan and I are doing and, I guess, to compare notes about the amount of ash that has fallen. We have all been planning to go to the Vue Pointe Hotel to celebrate Mother's Day with a barbecue lunch. We decide we should still go. We had not reckoned on the ash falling in Old Towne. Today I figure we eat as much ash as we eat food!

I know I have to do something more to really contribute to relieving the stress of my people. Carol Lawes's visit has sparked something in my imagination. Yes, we are doing an active programme of culture and the arts at the ten learning centres, but very little is being offered to the adults in the evening.

I realize that there are a lot of changes that may well affect us for the rest of our lives. To me, people seem angrier, less patient; I see more rum shops going up every day. Once, during the dry period, I was visiting my uncle and he was driving me around the island. He said, "The people of Montserrat are equally divided between the rum shop and the church. For every village have at least three churches and three rum shops."

Only now I see every street has at least six rum shops and no church, since the churches are all shelters. As I drive past a church-shelter one day, I slow down to look at what is happening. There are a group of men sitting under a tamarind tree playing dominoes. Actually, now that I reflect on it, I realize they have been there since April and it is now the middle of May.

An elderly gentleman swears at me and tells me to mind my *%**@** business! I am shaken up, despite the fact that I believe I should understand his reaction.

God has always blessed me by giving me really talented, creative and conscious friends. I mean they really care about what is happening to us. They are totally selfless.

God Will Find A Way is born out of the most dynamic and inspiring set of individuals that I have ever had the pleasure and joy of working with. One conscious sister, Sharon, one political activist and hard Rasta man, Atiba; one super writer, Jackie; one wacky comedian, Cepeekee, who loves talking to himself since then he is talking to a better class of people; one extempore calypsonian, Organizer, who also happens to be my zany uncle; one wickedly talented actress, Delacey; one true brother, Earl; and Rouselle, the Chief Minister's daughter – and I love them all.

We meet in my house one evening and a new family is created. We share our stories. Some are sad and others are very funny. One person still has not moved out of the unsafe zone. Some people still go home regularly to check on their houses.

Work is a nightmare for everyone. I don't know how I manage with the two jobs. Some people try to put pressure on me. I simply refuse to deal with them. I decide what my priorities are. Teaching the students is a priority. *God Will Find A Way* is a priority too.

We interview people in the shelters; we write poems and songs; we identify that the main problem for everyone is how to deal with the stress. We see the effects of that stress, and we try to show them in the production by highlighting the lighter side of things. We want to make people laugh. We want them to sing. We want them to be wary of some of the consequences of being confined to the shelters. We want them to believe that 'God will find a way'. But most of all, we want them to 'tek bad tings mek laugh.' And laugh they do. They roar at the butterfly poem. Actually the Chief Minister is in the audience on the opening night and he laughs too. But you know that you can never tell people's real thoughts.

Many people meet members of the group and tell us that looking at the production made them reassess their attitude to their situation. There is always someone worse off. We take the production to the shelters and there is always a packed crowd. One night we do the play in an Anglican Church. Another night we do the play in a large tent in Gerald Park. This tent is also used as a church. History is in the making. Church and theatre are reunited. This tent is a large tent and it is full. And when we finish, after one hour and fifteen minutes of performance, they ask us to do the whole play over again. Even those not living in the shelters come. They stand up and crane their necks to see *God Will Find A Way*.

We feel really good that we are making a real contribution. But my son tells me that while I am trying to relieve the stress of others, I am causing him stress. He resents the fact (and rightly so) that I spend so much time away from home. He resents the fact that I am otherwise dragging him everywhere. When he tells me that, I take stock. He certainly bursts my bubble. I realise we can change little. At the end of each performance, people still sleep in overcrowded shelters. They still queue up for bathrooms with strangers; still sleep in cots too small for them; still have to put up with the unfamiliar smell of people they have no desire to even talk to; still cannot make love in privacy; still are left wondering when will it all end.

One evening after a performance there is actually a fight. It seems that someone has touched another person's cot. The group feels powerless to do anything. The smell of uric acid in that shelter is so overpowering that everyone simply wants to leave. I start coughing so badly that I really need to leave.

We constantly review the production to reflect these incidents, so we continue to meet and review and rehearse. In the middle of rehearsing and performing, so much ash falls in Corkhill where we are rehearsing that life becomes more challenging. We constantly have to clean before we start. I can actually feel the ash at the back of my throat. I develop a cough that does not go away for months. We realize that it is impossible to work in the building that the government has given us to use. Soon the building is taken as a shelter. People need places to live. It is tiring. After nine weekends of performances, we take a well- deserved break.

Of course each time there is an *event* – by this time even I have caught on with the lingo – we consider it the worst one. Every time an ash cloud goes high into the air we wonder when she will go back to sleep. When is she going to stop? Everyone I know is stressed out. The laughter never stops, but people are beginning to make serious decisions to leave. Schools are in tents and all kinds of buildings, including restaurants.

I am still determined not to go anywhere. But when all the people I love start leaving and the ash keeps on pouring and the mountain keeps on blazing, I think it is time for a break. Life is pretty crazy at home. I am doing just about a million things. There is no peace or quiet. I am overworked and totally stressed out. I feel the Lord wants me to give my heart, body and soul. But it is also the most rewarding time of my life. I never knew before how fulfilling it is to truly give. I am so busy I have no time for myself. My son is suffering both psychologically and physically. He can't cope with the ash. He can't cope with me working so hard. But it is the ash fall of August 1, 1996 that finally makes me decide that enough is enough.

This day my cousin is travelling to Antigua with our grandmother, who is going to England. I get up really early in the morning to drive to the north to pick her up and get her organised for travelling. I really think that this is the best thing for my grandmother, since most of the family is in England. Besides, Laureen, who really spends most of the time dealing with her, needs a break so that she can get on with her own life.

But as my son gives his great-grandmother a farewell hug and they leave, my grandmother in a wheel chair, all my grandmother's words seem to turn in the wheels of that chair and echo in my head. At the point where they go through the door of departure, I remember. I remember shelling peas with her on her steps. I remember the piece of pumpkin and the breadfruit and the few green bananas that she "save for me in case me come out." I remember all the meals she made me carry to dark women in faded flowered dresses who had no teeth. I remember the walking stick she hit me with one day. I remember how she called me at 4 a.m. to tell me to listen to some radio programme about spiritual healing. I remember the stories she told me about puppa and mumma; about the old house at Jack Sweeney where she was born and about Aunt Fanny, her older sister, now dead. And the prayer she taught my son; and her childhood stories in which she was forced to work like a mule. How when my mother was born she was a beautiful golden baby and how she later turned out to be lazy and not like work. I remember the story she told me about why everyone called her Honey. I remember when I tried to plait her hair; the only one time she ever made me do it, she tell me how me hand too hard. I remember how she showed me how to pick the right aniseed and fevergrass bush to make tea. Showed show me how to crochet and hold the needle properly so that I don't look like a "monkey firing a gun". How she made me drive from town to the north to take her to church just so she could show everyone that her granddaughter had a new car. And how she corrected me every time I tried to speak dialect *because you is a big school teacher at the grammar school*. And I remember how she told me that she can't reach heaven on account of Hitler – the name she calls her husband.

In that moment, the world is still as she goes through the departure gate. This is all; these stories which will purify the soul. My son and I look up at the mountain. She is still there. Disturbing the leaves, the trees, the flowers, the sea, the animals, and all human kind. But she cannot take away those stories. No matter how hard she tries. And as the plane lifts off, I commit myself to my grandmother's stories. They are the stories of another world. Now the volcano would take that world away from me. If she only could.

My whole day is full of those stories. I begin immediately to share them with my son, who comes to work with me every day. It is lunchtime and we are driving home for lunch. We can see a huge pyroclastic flow coming from the East followed by a huge ash cloud. We have become so accustomed to seeing them, I stop the car at the Vue Pointe Hotel and we stand like everyone else to watch in fascination. This was a mistake. In no time at all the cloud is overhead. We jump in the car and reverse to drive in the opposite direction. I am sure that I can outdrive the ash. I can't. It starts pounding down on the car. I quickly pull onto Patsy's driveway, haul Nathan out of the car and run into the house.

We run straight into the bedroom at the back of the house. Suddenly there is darkness like the end of the earth. Darkness while the world is crashing. Even though there are eight of us in this room together, I feel a total solitude. This is all. I am a lone "bare forked animal". The world wails a loud lament. It crashes into my senses. The electricity goes off. More darkness. Radio Montserrat goes dead. The phone is dead. The children are all screaming. Sweat is pouring off me. Thunder and lightning pound. The ash is seeping through everywhere. Patsy is desperately trying to close all the windows. But the mountain manages to pour her dark mud over us. The mountain cracks. Crack crash. She mocks. Crack crash! She scolds. Crack crash! She shrieks. I remain surprisingly still, except for the odd time when I reach out to make sure I can feel everyone, especially Nathan. The darkness is such a total darkness that you can't even see the eyes or teeth of someone sitting right next to you. I don't know how long this lasts. But I hold my eyes firmly ahead. I cannot risk moving for fear that the mountain will get even angrier. As the black clouds carry the sun away, I cannot tell if the light that peeps its way into the darkness, into the stillness, into the mud, is the light which will return my muddy island to its old time, or whether this is the beginning of a new time. In this world of darkness time is endless. Now the mud comes down. I cannot even see where my yellow car is parked. More mud comes down. In this darkness I see all my life's bricks being washed away.

Later, much later, my son describes this experience as "a supernatural darkness". We are in St Thomas. The University of the Virgin Islands invites us to perform at their Folk Life Festival, all expenses paid if you please. *God Will Find A Way*. There is an American journalist filming the presentation. Nathan is playing the steel pan in between the scene changes. The journalist asks him about that August 1, 1996 event. "A supernatural darkness," he says. I don't know where he got that from and when I hear him say it, I am astonished.

Some limbs from trees are strewn across the road. Mud is everywhere. No one knows what has happened. But outside is covered in a black thick sludge of mud. The volcano batters us. It is as if the world is no more than defecation. Everyone is terrified and shaken. There are no words from any of us, no words at least for an eternity.

I begin to think seriously and deeply about life. I begin to think about fear. About how it can really motivate and propel a person into action. About all the things I haven't done with my life. The people I need to forgive. The people whose forgiveness I need. The people I owe letters. The people I love and whom I haven't properly told. In that terrible blackness, that blackness of mortality, that blackness which clutches at me, I begin to think about Jesus. I know that there's no point in panicking now. As I descend lower into these thoughts of blackness, I hear these words: "For unto us a child is born and He shall be called Jesus: for He shall save his people from all sins." So not my will but His will be done. But is it enough? Here in this darkness, is it enough? Yes. Now in this darkness, with the volcano pouring its ash and its mud down on us, I know that it is enough.

An hour later the radio comes back on. Ambeh tells us to remain indoors. To stay calm. I remember that the clothes I washed that morning are still on the line. I throw them all away the next day. They are caked with ash, mud and debris. I have to clear the ash from the verandah, from the roof; it has blocked the back door. I clean away ash and mud for the whole week. The following week there is so much ash outside my house that I apply for study leave, arrange my student loan and call the University of the West Indies to accept the place that they offered me earlier in the year.

I notice that Nathan really starts to wheeze. One day, things come to a head. I nearly come to blows with the entire health service. There is no medication at the nearest clinic. I can't find a doctor. I drive all the way to the north of the island to the hospital that is in a school that it has taken over. Only I discover, when I arrive, that casualty is in another building a mile away and I have driven past it on the way up. I meet an Indian doctor who barely understands my hysterical English. There isn't a native doctor in sight. The nurse eventually puts Nathan on a nebuliser, but we have had to wait for it since there is another child already using it who is equally sick. Then I have to leave him to go back to the original building to collect the medication. I wonder what happens to those sick people who do not have a car. It is the first time I feel spiders crawling under my skin. The whole experience is so tiring that I resolve there and then to leave. I feel this whole experience is likely to kill me before the volcano does. I resolve to leave at the end of the month.

My friend Patsy decides that she has to leave, too. I think she's fed up with the situation at school. Patsy is the most immaculate woman I know. She has been teaching under a dark green tent on the road going down to Salem Park. From April to the end of term the road is covered in ash. Cars speed by and the gusts of wind and ash blow into everybody's face, hair, nose and ears and their feet are white with ash. Patsy is not the kind of person who can tolerate being less than well dressed, especially at work. I hate to see the teachers working under those hot and dusty conditions. They are angry and frustrated. It is the best that can be done. The children are crowded and hot and irritable. Anyone would be hot and irritable if they got stuck in a hot, dark-green tent on sloping stony land that hurts your back, where the ground gets muddy when it rains and you have to sit on the desks, and you get wet because there are holes in the tents and the dust makes you cough and irritates your eyes when it is dry.

At home there is this interminable cleaning. No matter how hard I try I cannot get rid of the dust. I wash my toothbrush before I brush my teeth. I wash my comb before I comb my hair. I take out the chicken to defrost before cooking and in a few minutes it is covered in ash. I sit down to watch television and I am sitting in ash. The ash is all around me. Every morning before I go to work I wash off the car before I get in. One morning I decide to give my car a thorough cleaning; it is covered in enough ash to plant a field of sweet potatoes on it. I get distressed when I look at my car because it is relatively new: a bright yellow Toyota Starlet. The ash is seeping into the upholstery and it is beginning to look like a real banger, fit only for the knacker's yard. I finish cleaning it and the phone rings. It is Patsy. "Girl you see the pyroclastic flow coming down the mountain? The ash is coming straight towards you." When I put the phone down and go back outside, a grey powdery dust has already begun to fall lightly on the car. I watch with frustration and go back inside while the mountain does her thing. I do not clean the car again, merely clean the windscreen and windows and go off to work with the ash blowing all over. The pedestrians have a hard time. This cleaning thing is licking me and even though I say I will not be licked; I feel not only licked, but beaten.

I realise that I am sick of hearing "and now for your daily volcanic report." I am sick of seeing long lines of people queue up with yellow and green plastic bags for their rations of tinned and processed foods. I am sick of hearing the Government telling us that we are safe. And the Opposition telling us that we are not. I am sick of hearing the butterfly joke. I am sick of the noise of the helicopter waking me up every morning. I am sick of running outside to take my wet clothes off the line because ash is falling. I am sick of the dark circle of ash that seems to be perpetually over our village. I am sick of the smell of sulphur. I am sick of the constant taste of sulphur in the back on my throat. I am sick of seeing the garbage piled up. I am sick of the ash. I am sick of straining my neck daily to see that mountain. More than anything else, I guess I'm sick of the waiting:

the waiting to see whether our lives will ever get back to normal, the waiting to make plans for the future. I am sick of that mountain controlling my life. Life was so peaceful before the mountain.

So with everyone planning to leave, it seems futile to stay. It is not the fear of the volcano that really prompts me to go. It is the realization that the work I am doing can at best only help people to cope. It is the realization that the hospital is still in the school and the doctors are all planning to leave. For the first time in my life I am terrified of falling sick. It is the realization that school will never be the same again. So many teachers are leaving. My work, too, will soon be a distant and forgotten memory. With all the creative and talented people leaving, the work cannot sustain itself. It cannot heal. And we are in great need of healing – though that idea is only being whispered. We seem determined to show the world just how determined and fearless we are. In the end, I'm just plain tired. And when I look around and hear the loud and empty voices of politicians, I have a growing feeling of impotence. Impotence. It is a word I use every time I pass a shelter and hear that the British Government has promised millions of pounds to help relieve the plight and suffering of Montserratians.

Then the Governor announces that anyone who feels uncomfortable about remaining on the island can go to England for two years. The British Government promises to provide assistance when they arrive. Of course, you know I am NOT going to England. But a lot of my friends take up the offer. Of course, I don't blame them. Many of them are living in other people's houses, having a real hard time. The stories that people tell me are horrible. People locking their fridges at night. Hiding toilet paper. People can't even make love any more. Well, how can you make love in a shelter when in some cases the only thing separating you from your neighbour is a hospital screen. And then there are those stories about people who have their telephone bills rocket because they have someone living in their house. A girlfriend told me that no matter how much washing powder she bought, there was never any for her by the time she came to wash her clothes. People are really at the end of their rope.

The day Patsy, Jayenelle and Ortiz leave for England, I cry as if someone has died. The whole world seems to stop. I stand looking at the mountain. I watch that hateful, spiteful mountain that has interrupted my calm existence in Paradise. Nathan cries too. Actually, I should say he bawls. He bawls so much that he makes himself really sick. I rush home before the plane leaves so he can use his inhaler, which as usual, he has forgotten. I need to get away quickly. The whole airport seems to be awash with tears at Patsy's leaving. There is so much water that I nearly drown.

   Three weeks later I am on a plane. I am taking a year out. It has been an extremely difficult decision. So I think at the time. I don't realize then, of course, that there is a more difficult decision in store for me.

CHAPTER 4

My Study Leave

We leave Montserrat with suitcases and boxes and an assortment of odds and ends carefully chosen to tell our story. A picture of Nathan standing by the waterfall at Chances Mountain is the *piece de resistance*. Nathan cries all the way from the William H. Bramble airport at home till we arrive at the V.C. Bird International in Antigua. His sobbing is deep and quiet and long. I am sure his body is going to break. But really I believe this move is the best thing for him. A year will quickly pass. And besides, bodies don't break so easily.

I will get my well-deserved rest, and get my Masters in the process. Nathan will get a good foundation at a good secondary school. The first night we arrive in Barbados my son tells me that he doesn't mind staying here for a while, but Montserrat will always be his home. I feel so reassured by these words. Yes, we will eventually go back home. The mountain will go back to sleep. Just as she was before! That is my belief and my prayer. I feel so hopeful.

University life is like a summer breeze at first. I make some wonderful, supportive friends. I study real hard since I am determined not to waste my money. And I have a ball, too. I write poems. Being permanently broke makes no difference. I am determined to live my life to the full. I fret occasionally about Montserrat. I get angry occasionally at the pathetic news reports. Actually, I seem to have become a master at fretting. I wish I could get over that little foible. It really would save me some heartache. But my attitude through it all is that life goes on. I mean how much longer can this volcano business go on.

So I think that for now, Montserrat is behind me. Nathan thinks his new school is wonderful. But as far as we are both concerned, Montserrat will always be our home. But then one morning I am awakened at six o'clock by the ringing phone. I immediately think someone must have died. It is September 18. It is Warren, a fellow Montserratian. He seems out of breath.

He tells me there has been a huge explosion, that for the first time there are buildings on fire. Stones had actually came pelting through the air and reached the village of Corkhill. My home. The stones smash through houses in the village of Long Ground and car windscreens are shattered miles away. People run out of their houses in the middle of the night wearing their night things and run for their lives. With all their fancy, sophisticated machines, the scientists have once again been caught off guard. I call Laureen, my cousin. She has moved away to our grandmother's house. She tells me that there is no way she is going back.

So Corkhill is not safe after all. Yet the people remain even after this. Surely this is madness. I am relieved that my son and I left just in time.

University life is never quite the same after this. I begin to have slight doubts about whether I will really be able to go home at the end of the course. I have doubts that creep into my head whenever there is a news item on the radio or television. Just doubts. Slight.

I decide that I should really do something about the volcano as part of my course. My supervisor encourages all the overseas students to do our research project in our own countries. So, in January 1996, I go home. My son Nathan is very upset. I don't like the fact that he cries like a baby. Recently I find that he cries a lot. The truth is that when he was a baby he never cried. I mean, of course he cried, but not with tears or grief. To me he was the happiest baby in the world. Even his cries always had a smile. As far as the practicalities of my visit home there is no problem. My friends, Warren and Cleo, are quite wonderful. Even though they are both students, they offer to take care of Nathan for the two weeks that I am away. But I am disturbed by his reaction and begin to wonder how single mothers can make men out of their male children. This thought saddens me.

I stay in my grandmother's house in the north of the island. I am so busy doing my research that I hardly notice the volcano at all. Every day I interview teachers, parents and education officers in order to understand how they are managing the crisis. I talk to the students and have fun doing drama lessons. The school I am studying is in three tents pitched on a dusty, stony area. The wind and grass whips through everyone's hair. There are flies everywhere. Sometimes it is impossible to observe the classes because the flies and heat make it quite unbearable.

Around the school there are a number of shelters. There is so much noise I wonder how the staff and children manage. I hope that when I am finished analysing all the interviews and observations that my study will actually have some relevance to someone who has to manage a school in a crisis.

During this time I try my best not to get hooked on the volcano report. Most of my friends have left. There are one or two people who come to visit me at my grandmother's home and mostly we talk about the volcano. We talk about the research I am doing and what models of crisis management are emerging from the study. Most people are frustrated and believe that there will be a steady trickle of population out of the island. Mostly they are frustrated with the slowness with which help is coming from the rest of the world. They are frustrated about the fact that schools are still in tents. New buildings are being started but no one seems sure about when they will be finished. They are frustrated about the lack of homes for people still living in shelters. They are frustrated about the poor state of the hospital, still in a school. They are frustrated about everything.

The volcano itself does not seem to be the problem, even though it is still puffing and blowing. I am lulled into believing that all will soon be well – once the British release the millions of pounds we have been hearing about for so long. At least I will be able to go home at the end of the course. Maybe.

I decide to pay the Chief Minister a visit. I like him.

I consider him a gentleman and a man of integrity. Can you believe that the volcano blew in 1995 and from that time to now we have had three Chief Ministers? Anyhow, I tell him about my studies and my research. He tells me that he hopes I will be returning home at the end. Suddenly I realise that Montserrat has changed. And it is just not because of the volcano either. Well not directly. My grandmother always says there is no smoke without fire. I remember the talk about the racism at the Observatory, and you know there is not a single black scientist at the volcano observatory any more. The whole time I was making this visit home I realise that I don't hear a single black voice on the radio. I find it very strange that a whole heap of British scientists are talking about "we here" in Montserrat. I wonder what they mean by "we". I ask the Chief Minister about this. He just smiles. I tell him the British look like they take over the whole place, that I notice that they are driving a whole heap of cars that have H on the license plate. He smiles some more. Then suddenly I just blurt out that I have no intention of living on a plantation ever again. The meeting ends quite amicably. But he is, nevertheless, quite embarrassed.

Two days before I am due to return to Barbados, my cousin and another friend decide to go to Tar River. Now, we know it's dangerous. There are warnings on the radio from the scientists that no one should set foot in the area. This warning is on every day. At least six times a day. But Laureen and I are curious. We do not once think about curiosity killing the cat. Instead, my friend decides that since he is from the East, he knows the mountain better than any scientist does and nothing is going to happen. He is one of those *diehards* who refused to move from the village of Long Ground. And even though the water and electricity have been cut off for some time now, he refuses to live in a shelter or move in with anyone else.

"Yvonne!" he cries repeatedly, whenever I admonish him for remaining up there. "How me a go live? Me no eat tin food and dem things there! The government a go feed me what me accustom to?"

So we drive up to the Tar River house that is now burnt, with only the columns remaining. I don't recognise the place because the green turrets of Castle Peak's mountain are gone. Instead, there is a ghostly white sea of ash sprawling like a desert as far as the eye can see. Nowhere is there a single sign of life. Not even a butterfly. It is like nothing you can ever imagine. There are no more valleys and no more mountains. There are no more trees or leaves. There is no more land to walk on. The riverbed, which once rushed with clear spring water, is gone. And the white goes out to the sea and covers the sea. There is steam coming out of the ground, which we know we must not touch because it is supposed to be about 300 degrees centigrade. Never have I laid my eyes on such a stark, barren – or beautiful – piece of Earth. It is like a waking dream. We are all hypnotised by the immensity and austerity of what we see. It is both breathtaking and tranquil.

Voices jolt us back to reality. The voices belong to white scientists who warn us to go back and we do so quickly and quietly. My friend says, "You see that all a you a run. And all you a left the country to the white people and dem to take over." My cousin Laureen tells our friend, "You mad to stay up in Long Ground. Not me." We drop him home and drive back to the north of the island. I decide that he has the heart of a lion. As for me, I tremble all the way back to my grandmother's house. As I shake the grey dust from off my feet, I feel as if I have seen the eighth wonder of the world.

It does not dawn on me until the next day, when I tell my friend John about my visit, what an irresponsible thing we have done. That very night there was an explosion and lava flow down the mountain. John is very angry with me. He reminds me that I have my son to live for. He asks me to put the mountain behind me. I take his concern to heart. Imagine if the mountain had coughed then. She would have melted my scalp. I need to remember that the mountain is not only beautiful, but deadly. Besides, I don't want to die so young and beautiful.

I return to Barbados and I wonder if I ever want to go back to Montserrat. It is really significant to me that all the black scientists have left Montserrat, and that, as far as I can see, everything on the island is being run by the British. Then I feel like a traitor and push such thoughts behind me. Back to University work.

June 25th is a fateful dark day for me and for every Montserratian. It is the day the volcano kills nineteen people. I hear the news at about two twenty on Liberty FM. It is the most devastating news I have ever heard in my life. I panic. There are three people with whom I am very close who work at the airport and I need to make sure they are all right. I call home, but I can't reach my uncle. I immediately call Warren, my "adopted son", who is home for the summer-break from UWI. As usual his response is nonchalant. He assures me that the news is exaggerated. "Girl, don't panic," he says.

Of course he is wrong, as he later admits. As usual the outside world knows more about what is happening than people at home. That day the phone never stops ringing. I call home at least a dozen times, oblivious to the expense. I am so glad that my cousin Laureen is not home. She is in London getting married. I wonder how she is feeling. I speak to my friends, Lowell and Gary and Salas, who call me at times throughout the next day to keep me informed of all that is happening. Tears fall in large lumps. That night I cannot sleep. I scream the loudest scream I have ever screamed. Of course, I am careful not to disturb the neighbours. So no one hears me.

I discover that everyone is fine and "got out just in time". It is a phrase I keep hearing, but I cry relentlessly for three days. Eventually, my friend Lowell gets me to snap out of it by explaining that I am suffering from the Montserrat disease. At night I am haunted by the faces of the people I know who have lost their lives, their homes, their loved ones. I feel helpless and powerless. There is a stillness in me. It is deeper than grief. I am wondering why, when I call home, everything seems to be happening as usual. Yes life must go on. But I wonder when the healing will begin, when we will stop laughing to hide the pain?

So there is no going back home. I have no home to

go back to any more. Corkhill is now designated unsafe, as I always believed it was. I have to regroup. I have to make plans. I need air to think. The course will soon be over. The money is almost gone. I have to decide what I am going to do. Memories of England come back to me. The dry period. No matter how hard I try, I do not have any good memories. I imagine there must have been some. But I remember the cold. I remember four guys spitting on me from a car. I remember the cold summers. Once, I remember having to walk quickly when I got off the bus for fear of being attacked by a white boy wearing army boots. I remember the damp cold. I remember my car breaking down on a cold December morning, my son, only six months old, crying out his lungs and every one passing by me on the road. I remember the bitter winters. I remember the smell of paraffin, and peeling wallpaper and the Tottenham riots where a policeman was hacked to death. I remember fighting to be seen and heard. I remember that there is no sun. England is completely out of the question. It is a country I fear.

My family, though, want me to return to England. As if somehow the streets of England have finally decided to proffer up the gold they were reputedly paved with all those years ago when my parents came off the ship in the 50s. But then I think about all they have endured, and I know if I go back there, where I will never see mountains, or dewdrops on leaves, or men hanging out with their chests glistening with sweat, my longing for Montserrat will be unendurable. In England there could be no replacement for the Evergreen Tree where I once discussed politics with the guys, and I would never again feel the golden tropical sunlight that creeps slowly over you in the morning when you are lying in the luxury of a lover's arms.

I thank God for giving me my friend Cynthia at this time. She is a student on my course. From Antigua. She is the only person who truly understands my dilemma. I spend a lot of time with her and she is really good for me because she reminds me that I am truly blessed. When I talk to her about the mountain she really believes in my ability to overcome all difficulties.

Life goes on. A man invites me out to supper one night. He takes me to Cheffette, which is like – FAST FOOD! And he takes me to the Cheffette on Nelson Street, which is like Soho or Brixton or Trenchtown, depending on your perceptions of ghettos. We park his fancy CD registration car and prepare to eat. Only I don't. Because I'm much more fascinated with the "sketels", the hookers who are walking by outside. At one point I wonder if someone is going to steal his four tyres like they do in gangster movies. This might just be the highlight of my night!

Finally, I meet a man whom I think is real. I start relating to him in early 1997. Please note I say re-la-ting. Once, I try explaining to this man the terrible plight of Montserratian families who have been separated as a result of the volcano. I try to explain how their losses are both physical and psychological. I try to explain how difficult it is to start again from scratch. I try to explain the difficulty of starting when you have nothing to start with. I fail to explain well.

"Don't lament!" he says. I can't believe what he is telling me.

"Life is about new beginnings," he rambles on. "Look at me. I have just spent $7,000.00 dollars (U.S. of course) to set up an apartment in New York."

I didn't even have 700 pennies at that moment. But this was going to be my man. He had seemed to have all the qualities I was looking for. How wrong can a woman get?

This was the man I was hoping, assuming, expecting to help me get over this crisis. He was, after all, a psychologist. But then I learn that it is dangerous to assume that psychologists have their own lives together, and that however good you assume they might be at analysing everyone else, the only thing this one was really good at was explaining away his own faults with some stupid psychological theory. It was unjust. I had never lamented to this man. In fact, in all the time I had related to him (his words not mine), he had never seemed to be in the least bit concerned about how I was coping with having to leave my home and settle here. He knew I had not worked for nearly a year, but he never asked me once how I was getting through or adjusting to the situation at home. So much for psychology. I learn a lot of psychology from the mountain.

Months later I think about this selfish, insensitive, arrogant man and I wonder how I could have thought that he would really understand. I guess I was clutching at straws. When I think about the fact that he never once offered to help me either practically or emotionally, I write a poem. I decide to send him a copy, hoping

that once he reads 'Bread' he will know exactly what
I think of him and he can just go his funky way:

Flashing his false teeth in my face,
his big head shining like a dome,
he comes with his sweet mouth
and sugars up my ears
with promises of gold and distant places
when all I want is bread.

He squeezes his fat stomach
into a pair of Dockers jeans
and his two, too big feet
splat! splat! on my carpet
which I'd just paid $1.00 deposit on.
"You are a part of me!" he declares,
but all I want is bread.

He touches me in places
he'd recently discovered from reading
101 ways to Make Love to a Woman,
places I already knew I had.
"All that I have is yours," he whispers,
but all I want is bread.

He looks at me through
too-dark glasses and flattens me
with his once virile body.
"You're so lovable and cuddly and warm."
I wonder why all the clichés?
Since my fridge is empty,
all I want is bread.

I want bread and peace and quiet. Bread and hope. Bread and safety. Bread with the mountain far away. The smell of fresh-baked bread and the feeling of home. It is a good thing I never put this man at the centre of my life. It is a good thing that it is God I put there. Even though I admit that my faith wavers like a pendulum, I get through because I have faith. I pray. I don't mean that I go to church. And I don't just suddenly *find* religion. I know that God will provide all my needs and that whenever I let go of this faith, stop praying, I get depressed and everything goes wrong.

The mountain is doing her thing again. I'm doing my thing too. CBC and CANA start spouting off daily and the volcano within me starts raging. I realise that the only way I am going to survive in this new island is if I pray. So I sit down on the floor, on my bed, on the toilet, wherever, and just ask God to provide all my needs. And He does, though I am not worthy, I am not worthy.

So it doesn't matter that not a single member of my family understands the loss I feel, because after one whole year of living on an island without family, without earning a living, of wondering whether I will ever have my home again, with no one … Mother… Father… Aunt… Uncle… Cousin… ever asking me if I need a dollar to buy a loaf of bread, I know that there's no valley that I can't cross, no river I can't wade across, no mountain that's too high – and so the clichés go on.

But why the hell did I ever want to turn to any of these people anyway? Whenever I talk about family, Warren always reminds me that a family is just a group of people living in the same house and sharing the same privileges. He claims that he learnt this in Social Studies, a subject that I always found to be absolutely boring, but which he (Warren!) manages to make applicable to my situation.

   I know I really shouldn't feel alone because I'm always getting little notes from people I haven't been in touch with for a while, but they're usually from people that I don't feel particularly close to. People call, but it's always because they want some favour. They want a ride from the airport to the American Embassy or they have some papers they want me to pick up from there. Or they want a bed for the night so they can sort out their visas or pick up the passports that have been at the Embassy for weeks. And then, when they come, the only talk we really have is about her, the mountain.

   I am getting used to the love and support of strangers, like Blanche in *A Street Car Named Desire*. Only I'm determined not to end up in the lunatic asylum as she did. But this state of things could drive me crazy. There are days when I feel suspended like a balloon, drifting, drifting in the upper atmosphere. The world seems to have stopped. There are days when I feel faceless. Even when I look in the mirror I can't see myself. But the mountain is always there. She is there growing bigger and refusing to go away. I think she must have caught the plane. She's following me everywhere.

   Writing helps. I write a poem about how I really feel. I remember once hearing a certain gentleman, a famous poet and historian, saying that too many people were calling themselves poets who didn't know anything about structure and form. Well, I learnt plenty about structure and form from the neo-colonial education that I had. But I didn't learn one thing about my story. Or how to write about a mountain that haunts you even in your sleep. Nor did I learn anything about how to express the social, cultural and psychological handicaps of the black woman. So I decide I can write anything that releases me from those oppressions, including the ones the poet-historian wants to create with his insistence on structure and form. So I write. Audaciously, defiantly, I write.

CHAPTER 5

Can you see my country burning?

At night my son and I couldn't sleep for the walls would shake and the night air seemed to tremble with the mountain's rumblings.

The world was being peeled open like a huge orange and the sky was aflame with black smoke from the mountain's rumblings.

The mountain exploded, spilling her guts out over Long Ground where no one ever went but where cars nightly parade to see the mountain's rumblings.

The dust settled on my house and my car, on every thing I owned like unwanted dandruff and I learned to clean away daily the mountain's rumblings.

Mother's day came and the day turned into night as the volcano bellowed a large belch reminding us that it was not the politicians who were in control of the mountain's rumblings.

They crammed my people into shelters – churches once holy, now only fit for pigs, to protect us they say from the terrible wrath of the mountain's rumblings.

And so the people fled; some like Lot's wife couldn't bear to leave, remembering only the once silent, verdant views now turned to stone by the mountain's rumblings.

Can you hear the moan of a people displaced and dispossessed and wandering in the heat of a volcano that would not let them be with its rumblings?

Can you see my country burning?
Can you see her dying?
Can you hear her moaning?
Can you hear her?
moaning
moaning
moaning
moaning
m-o-a-n-i-n-g

The mountain is my muse. But writing this poem doesn't stop me from being angry at what has happened. There is a lot of talk about blame. Soon after these terrible events, a Barbadian girlfriend of mine calls me to express her concern about the Montserrat situation. She tells me that she had invited a Montserratian teacher to stay with her at her home for a few days. When my friend asked about Montserrat, the picture she drew for her was that everything was fine. My friend tells me that based on what this teacher said she was unsure about whether there was actually a crisis in Montserrat. When I was younger and lived in the dry period, they used to say that snow had gone to our brains. The mountain has surely gone to a lot of people's brains.

No one was supposed to die from this volcano. At least, so I thought. I call my good friend Warren C. fairly often during these times even though, God knows, I can't afford these calls. His response makes me even more disheartened. He says "the government told them not to go in the area and they refused to listen". The dead, then, are to blame for their own deaths.

I am still in a state of shock, anxious about those who are left, anxious about those who have left. I am continually being reminded that I can go back to England.

"No thank you," I say.

I know the racism of the British. It is perpetual and pervasive. This is evident from their treatment of Montserratians both in Britain and in Montserrat. The mountain has left me in a state of imbalance. She has fragmented me. I need to find the Evergreen Tree.

The mountain inspires me. Over the next few weeks while writing up my research project, I read everything I can get my hands on about crisis management. I have ordered at great cost articles, research journals, books from Britain, America and Canada. I plough through documents produced by Caricom and CDERA. I am determined to produce a document that will actually be significant in years to come. All I read confirms what I instinctively know. Those who *must* be blamed for the deaths are those who failed to manage the crisis. It is too simple to blame the mountain.

I wonder how many of the people responsible for *managing* the crisis actually understood the meaning of the word? I mean did they understand the issues of crisis management? Did they understand that the main principle of crisis management is to provide for the orderly movement of people to places where the danger is minimal? Did they understand that in a crisis no one person has all the answers? Did they understand the concept of the team approach? Did they understand that roles need to be rotated because the managers themselves will experience the crisis and may show "greatly reduced cognitive functioning in the areas of memory, concentration, articulation of thoughts and organization and planning ability"?

By not providing adequate alternative homes (why are we calling them shelters?), every single manager of this crisis failed to understand the "enormous psychosocial and practical importance of homes." Why had homes been built which were still unoccupied? Why had homes been built which had no toilet facilities? Why had certain individuals kicked up a fuss because homes were being built near their castles? Which one of these managers would be prepared to live in an overcrowded shelter like a pig for over two years? Did these managers really care about the dignity of the lives of Montserratians? I felt strongly that the money being spent each month to provide certain managers with comfort and luxury was unethical and immoral. Which of the managers was responsible for the decision to build the wooden shacks in Little Bay? Was it one of Her Majesty's managers? Or was it a locally elected manager? Or one of the technical managers? Wasn't

Little Bay earmarked for something grander than a new ghetto? Or were previous plans no longer viable? Is Montserrat viable? Is the mountain to be blamed for everything?

Working long hours is not crisis management. Building a school that cannot be accessed is not crisis management. Building homes without the infrastructure for access is not crisis management. Allowing government tractors to plough land in the unsafe zone is not crisis management. Buying food from the same farmers who were killed is not crisis management. Having food rot in containers is not crisis management. Allowing the airport to be open on a day when there was extreme heightened activity is not crisis management.

"And I hear the governor run for he life too. So I hear."

Providing food vouchers and a cot is not crisis management.

"And I hear too that some people saving up their vouchers and planning to get rich on those same vouchers."

Making trips in order to beg for more money for Montserrat is not crisis management. "And I wonder when we going stop begging?"

Not discussing *all* contingency plans with *all* of the people of Montserrat is not crisis management.

"And I hear that they say that all of us know what those contingency plans are. Really?"

Having a ferry as the main means of exit from Montserrat in the middle of a hurricane is not crisis management. Going on regional radio and telling the Caribbean that Montserratians are coping well is not crisis management.

I hear the mountain laughing at us. I hear her laughing at us. I hear her laughing real loud. You see the mountain not easy at all. Not easy at all.

The present set of managers need to acknowledge that their mismanagement is the cause of the mass exodus of Montserratian people from the island. It is their mismanagement that has caused more lasting harm to Montserrat than the Langs Soufriere. The picture of a young Montserratian boy in the July 1997 issue of the *National Geographic* epitomizes the nonchalant attitude of these managers to this crisis. What a damning message to send out to the rest of the world! The managers of a crisis must inspire confidence in their community. The present managers have failed, and many of them are now sitting comfortably – ash free – back in Britain, aided and abetted by a handful of our own people. They are to be blamed for the death of every individual who lost his life on that fatal day. But they are only human. And there but for the grace of God go I.

For as I ask myself all these questions, I know the answers are more complicated. And stuck as I am in Barbados, away from the events, there is really no one to answer me. What can I do to make a difference? These are the thoughts that go charging through my mind. I know these are strong words, but I feel as if we've all been hiding behind fear. Right or wrong we have to say what's in our hearts.

At other times I just feel lost, because I simply do not know. I'm not there. I conclude it is probably almost as bad being away as being home. It's certainly just as confusing, bewildering and frustrating. But I just don't know. All I know is that my island is sinking. People I once knew have been burnt beyond recognition. I begin to wonder if there will be anything left. I feel a great nothingness, a nothingness that hollows me, an emptiness that shrouds me. Shrouds my vision. A vision of skulls comes to me one night. All the bodies that once lay in their polished mahogany tombs wander the white desert land. The ground is opened up. The bridges are all crushed. Every leaf has been swept away. My spirit wanders through this desert. It tries to find the Evergreen tree, but the earth is melted hot and I cannot find a resting place. I watch helplessly as those skulls are crushed into dust. Graves can no longer be tended. It makes me think about hell and fire and eternal damnation more than ever.

CHAPTER 6

The Evergreen Tree

Finally, I decide to settle here in Barbados. Flat and without mountains. But where she can't find me. Langs. And without ash either. The British Government announces that it will help people who wish to resettle in other islands in the region with the sum of $10,000 E.C. for adults and $2,500 for children under 18. I think these figures are ridiculous. Who is going to help those of us who have lost everything? Mr. B. Osborne, resigns as our Chief Minister and Mr. David Brandt becomes Chief Minister of four thousand people! Prisoners walk out of the old library that someone decided to call a prison. Julian Romeo, a young local businessman, is on television every day leading protests against the inadequate compensation being offered by the administrators for homes and businesses. The volcano has everyone heated and in a frenzy. Finally, people are beginning to see the mountain for what she really is. She is the total destruction of our lives. I watch all of this on CBC, and *The Nation* carries stories almost everyday. It is now August 1997. God smiles on me, and a hundred Hail Marys later, I get a job teaching Theatre Arts at the Barbados Community College. I find an unfurnished house and wait patiently for the money to come from the British High Commission. It never comes.

Actually what comes is exactly $441.00 Barbados dollars to be paid every two months over a six month period for my son. This is reparation. The British government thinks it is enough. To replace all memories of home and land and friends? To replace the books collected over years of reading and travelling? To replace the crocheted blanket that my mother made with her own arthritic hands? To replace my Saturday afternoon retreats to my grandmother's and my Tan Tan's houses? To replace spoons, forks, pans, plates, sheets, brooms, cups, dishes, pictures of Mama, the mango tree where I relax with my son, the closeness of neighbours who care, my little yellow car which I never once locked? To root myself in a foreign land? To replace the Evergreen Tree! I wonder if the mountain has planned this. She must be in cahoots with the British.

I should not have been surprised or disappointed. The British have never cared. Instead of evacuating the people of Montserrat to safety, Governor Savage comes on the radio and says, "If you are not comfortable with the situation, then leave." So most of us spent our little savings and fled the island. I'm sure they must be smiling now. It cost them nothing. Savage, and that pompous Clare Short and her talk about golden elephants and that very minor John Major, and the FCO, the ODA, the BDD and all the "other planners and implementers for colonial policy" (as I read in Cheddy Browne's article on the internet. Much respect). All these people are making plans about our lives and

I don't even know what those abbreviations stand for. I feel that they are all smiling as they sing, "See how they run! See how they run". Actually, I still haven't figured out what all those letters mean. And I don't care, because I know that at the end of the day the mountain is still in control.

I set up house and this is difficult with so few dollars to start with. I mean I didn't have $7,000 US. Remember? I haven't "knocked a stroke" for the last twelve months. All I have been doing is studying. People do offer to help. There is this man. He has this big-up important regional job. He offers to lend me a bed. Well I figure that's real generous of him, because I never pick up any vibes that he's expecting something in return. (And if he is, then he is certainly going to be disappointed.)

Well, the day I move into this house I arrive with the rest of my things and there's this bed leaning up under the garage against the wall. I can't quite figure it out. I mean this man is a real neat and immaculate man. I figure he wouldn't go buying anything from the Salvation Army or a jumble sale. But there's this bed: old, broken down, filthy rusty, dilapidated, which most likely had seen better times during World War II, the kind with springs which I wouldn't give a sick dog to sleep on. I wonder if I am supposed to be grateful. Then I figure for the first time that I am well and truly an evacuee and he has devalued me, one time. But this is one period of my life when I know I must truly value myself because, let's face it, the mountain has scatted us and we are out there meeting hell, and I know I have to hold onto my dignity and my self-respect if I am going to survive.

So I don't tell a soul that the first month that I start working I hardly eat. In fact, I actually eat lunch, which consists of either two bananas or an apple, only four times that whole month. After buying some basic household necessities, I had just enough money to get to work and feed my son – and even that I could only accomplish through the genuine kindness of a few significant individuals. The people who *offered* to help me were the people I least expected. I thank God for Gary and the Grahams and Adrian and Jackie. I thank God for Terry who fixed the old banger and waited without ever harassing me about his money, and who has remained a loyal and faithful friend. I lose about fifteen pounds weight that month and I'm looking like a rake. I'm grateful that my mother cannot see me. If my grandmother could see me now, well, she would be sure to tell me that my collarbone needed porridge. I don't tell my family in England any of this, for it would have really given them the excuse to go on and on about me coming back there. Sometimes I cook just enough food for Nathan, who eats as much as any two hundred pound man. If he leaves any food, then I eat. I did not complain once. I did not want to give the mountain that satisfaction.

At work I find myself losing all sense of direction and identity. The coldness of people keeps me in a state of deep freeze. I feel utterly rejected by both the people and my surroundings. I feel as if I am in a state of shock but with no one to share my pain. I become suspicious of everyone around me and afraid to share my feelings with them in any way. I become paranoid. Everything causes me pain. My nerves are raw.

I notice that I don't laugh any more. I try to recall when this happened. I can't. But I know that my body no longer shakes from the depth of laughter the way it used to under the Evergreen Tree, the real laughter that used to tickle the inside bottom of my stomach and lift me up. Nothing anyone says or does seems funny. Before, no matter how badly the mountain behaved, there was always laughter. Somehow this made things much clearer. Then laughter always seemed to empty me of all my anger and frustrations. I could put things into their proper perspective. I don't know where the laughter has gone. I only know that even when I am surrounded by laughter, I don't hear it.

Once again I feel my faith in God lapsing. I know I cannot allow this feeling to continue. I am in a deep blue funk. During this time I read only three books which really give me any strength and sustenance, and which I read repeatedly. The book of Job in the Bible, Khalil Gibran's *The Prophet* and a book which Jackie lends me called *Feel the Fear and do it Anyway* by Susan Jeffers. Even though I know I do not have Job's qualities, I feel that I know just what he was going through. I wish I could be as upright and good as Job. I decide that this book must have been written just for me. My grandmother always used to say that no bad wind ever blows. I now know exactly what she means. Before this thing happened, I gave God very little thought, or I only thought about Him when I needed something, or when things weren't quite going my way. Now I thank Him every day for my blessings. I even thank Him for all the toxic people who have come in my life, who teach me that the world has many colours.

Even though I feel the pain is building up, I know that everything must change and nothing stays the same. This too will pass. I thank Him because I realize that if I look deep inside, I can see Him right there, reminding me of my essential goodness, reminding me that He will bless me. Perhaps the mountain just wanted to teach me a lesson about God and my own essential goodness.

Khalil Gibran says that it is well to give when asked, but it is better to give unasked, through understanding. I can't quite keep my eyes upon God all the time, even though I believe I should, but the Evergreen, that tough, old tree which could not be uprooted, is forever on my mind. With her wide girth that could not be contained, she was forever watching over me. Strong and powerful and unbending. I don't think even that other 'she' could topple her.

I think all the time: where is home for a Montserratian person? What is to become of us? Scattered and dispersed all over this world, we have become a landless people, living in conditions that we could never have imagined. Houses burnt. Land burnt. Possessions destroyed. Animals gone. Friends gone too, perhaps never to be seen again. People dead. Second-class citizens in another man's country. I am not prepared to be a second-class citizen anywhere, though this what I am described as by one of my students whose opinions, knowledge of the world and experiences are limited to Barbados. I am thankful that Barbados is not the world. I know that even though I have seen a lot more of the world than she has, there is so much more to be seen, and that whether or not I am a first or second-class citizen is dependent on my image of myself and not on anyone else's. Since I am created in God's image, I can't be a second-class citizen anywhere.

Meanwhile, the people of Montserrat struggle. They have to sleep on cots that are too small for them, and do not get even enough assistance to buy a refrigerator. Nothing. Nothing. The whole assistance deal is a scam, a fraud. I feel now that there can never be any kind of reconciliation between the British oppressors and Black people anywhere in this world. All this time we've been singing 'God save Our Gracious Queen' and saluting the Union Jack on the Queen's birthday. And Britons never, never shall be slaves. But we are not British. We're Montserratians. Or rather we are British Dependent Territories Citizens. A mouthful.

I receive a letter that goes something like this: I regret to inform you that because of the level of your stated regular income you are ineligible to receive assistance under the scheme. Blah! blah! blah! Wow I'm rich. That is why I eat my meals on a cushion on the floor, why my clothes are packed in suitcases, and why I have no furniture.

This is a very humbling experience. But through it all I know I must acknowledge my blessings. I have a wonderful son; I am able to work and I am constantly aware that my ability to start again is being watched over by God. Each day becomes easier. If I only look, I can see I am overflowing with abundance. I am blessed. I fight to come out of the cave and carve my own space.

The thing is *not* to expect people to care. Some will anyway. *Not* to expect people to understand. Some do.

There are nights when I don't sleep well, when I can't be sure if the next explosion will be the last one, the one that will completely obliterate everyone I know. The people that you *expect* to care often can't deal with these feelings. It's as if there is a wall of silence, like death. It is uncomfortable and unnerving. It is often the people you meet in the ordinary course of daily living who will show real compassion and understanding. One day I go shopping at the Sheraton Plaza. I don't even own a teaspoon or a cup, so I buy a whole set of kitchen and bathroom stuff. I mention to the shop assistant that I am relocating from Montserrat and she quickly arranges for the manager to give me a ten percent discount, which I promptly thank God for. But then a friend whom I really care about tells me that the problems Montserratians are experiencing are no different from what everyone has to go through. This friend always seems to have her life completely together, but as I am talking to her about home, she suddenly blurts out that she has her problems too. She tells me that her best friend's house has just been put up for auction and that she has heard about it from the newspapers and how terrible that must be for her friend. She, too, has problems with her man that she can't talk about and that her mother is manipulative and trying to control her life. Naturally, I sympathize with her because my best friend Patsy's house in George Street has just been burnt to the ground by pyroclastic flows.

There is, of course, some truth in what my friend says. I don't know one black woman who has hasn't experienced the emptiness and the untruths of some deceiving black man, and I certainly know how manipulative mothers can be because I removed the halo from mine a long time ago. Even though I feel she misses the point about the enormity of what Montserratians have gone through, her tone of resentment wakes me up. I realise it is high time I put Montserrat behind me and stop running up my phone bill calling people who never call me back. But not before I write just one more poem, giving this friend a piece of my mind.

My deepest memories are being burnt away
    one by one;
my childhood gossip buried in an avalanche
    of billowing ash.
You cannot understand that at night a tiny grain
    of dust in my bed can awaken me,
though it is merely innocent fluff that has settled.
I should feel safe, but I don't; I am in a foreign land
    and homeless.
They've told me that I am welcome here,
    but your prayers are rarely for me.
I am too close.
Bosnia is much safer.

I search for and sometimes find smiling
    and welcoming faces,
but you cannot understand the pain or the terror
    I have in dreams.
As my island goes up in smoke, taking with it
    my sister's house,
my once treasured haven; and the smoke of the church

where I once worshipped and taught my son to pray,
    wafts up to heaven,
my heart is drowned in a blaze of fire.
    When you speak of your recent marital tiff –
a mundane expression of everyday living
    (of which I too can speak) –
and your mother's death or mine,
    I understand as part of all human experience,
but the flagellation of my country, where nothing
    will grow, you cannot understand.

You cannot understand the terror I feel even
    with the rising sun,
the fear that everyone I know has vanished and
    no graves are marked,
that the laughter of farmers whose produce
    I once quibbled over
has been silenced in an avalanche of flames.
I am afraid to think of all that emerald turned
    to deathly white.

You cannot understand that my Evergreen Tree,
    where once I argued politics,
can never grow again, nor crown my head
    with its majestic splendour.
You tell me instead of your small pains.
I remain silent.
I have learnt to scream quietly.
I've been practising for two years.
Even my son lying next to me can't hear my cry,
though his own pierces the air.
He thinks too often of home,

his family and friends, scattered in distant lands. You say you care. But I cannot hear you.

    I can only read your lips.

Of course, I'll never show her the poem because I would really hate to hurt her feelings. She has been very supportive of Nathan and me throughout the year in real practical ways, and that's rare in this country. But I did get a chance to perform the poem in St Vincent at the Hairoun Theatre concert in September 1997, which was being held to raise funds for the people of Montserrat. And there was this deafening silence when I had finished, followed by thunderous applause. Not even the sound of the mountain could compete with that. So there!

    I perform the poem again, here, at 'Word Up', a poetry reading organized to celebrate Barbados' independence. It has a strange effect on a lady in the audience who is also a poet. She is reading after me. She says she finds it difficult to read her own poems after such a poem. She is a beautiful ebony black woman with locks on her head. Statuesque with a smile which radiates warmth, a warmth I have never noticed here before. I am astonished at this realization. After hearing her speak, I want to escape as I realize that the poem is an indictment of something that to some extent I now no longer feel. To some extent. She asks me not to leave. So I stand rooted to the spot as she speaks about her own feelings about the loss of Montserrat. My throat is dry and I am desperate for a glass of water. She reads a poem about the islands of the Caribbean. She dedicates it to "the sister from Montserrat". To me. I stand mesmerized. Eyes wander from the performer to the sister. From her to me. I consider the power of poetry. The feeling is reciprocal. Despite the bed incident, there are people who care.

  I want to tell her how much I appreciate her, but we pass each other like two tugboats and we make no contact. It is this lack of contact that makes me think about home where people forever touch, whether to love or fight. I wonder what could have happened to these people to make them so cold and dispassionate. Why they feel they have to hide the natural God-given sunshine that I know He gave to all Caribbean people? It is this that makes it impossible for me to put Montserrat behind me.

One day I am watching *Sesame Street* with my son – he is the sun – and one of those puppet characters is singing a song 'London Bridge is falling down', except the words are different. And through the aloneness this makes me feel, I start to write. I decide to write a short story. I call it 'Beloved'. I get the title from a book I have just finished reading by Toni Morrison. But over the months the story gets longer and longer. Then I call it 'The Final Passage'. Then I call it 'Testimony', because I realise that this is exactly what it is. I write every day feverishly and fervently. There is this fire in my brain, which cannot be extinguished. The ash cannot cover it. In fact it fuels my energies. And though my body and my heart feel this great loss, my mind is alight.

  Demons take over. I remember Miss Gwen sitting in town long after everyone has been relocated. She

refuses to move and sits on a concrete step with her
back to the mountain. I imagine her voice singing. And
I become her.

"Plymouth Town is burning down
Burning down
Burning down
Plymouth town is burning down
I am the fearless lady."

FIRE!
But Miss Gwen was not moving.
Moving?
Moving?
She wanted to stay.
She felt she could outroar any mountain.
She had faced demons in her dreams,
demons with large yellow fangs
who came to her bearing gifts:
gold, frankincense and myrrh.

Fire!
She had faced demons in the schoolyard,
demons with bright red ponytails
who came and kicked her, tripped her
for being too bold, too black, too beautiful.

Fire!
She'd faced demons in her husband's drunken
      face at night,
felt their feet stomping her face;
She'd faced them from her sisters' lying tongues

who smiled to her face, then pounded that
 face in the dust.
She'd faced them in the unborn faces
of all those children she had flushed away.

Fire!
She'd faced them in a cool bottle of rum
which made all the demons disappear.
Fire?
She threw back her head and she laughed.

"Plymouth town is burning down
Burning down
Burning down
Plymouth town is burning down
I'm the fearless lady".

It is my son who makes me understand that I am fearless. Now I marvel that he always seems happy. I admire his resilience. All his earlier tears have dried up and been turned to laughter. I wonder where he gets his strength. He says simply, "Mum, everything is going to be alright." His face lights up like the sun. One day he calls me an African Queen. Another day he says, "Mother, remember who you are. You're Yvonne Weekes."

But no matter how hard I try, I cannot put Montserrat behind me. My soul is caught up with this island. I feel totally disconnected here in this cold country where the sun always shines. I have begun to experience a kind of loneliness that shakes my body continually. It tugs at where my heart is supposed to be. I am losing touch with my ancestral spirits. I didn't realize, until now, just how important the land was to me. I did not realize, until now, just how much of what I am is connected to that rich black soil and those saw-toothed mountains. Over the past few months I begin to see myself separate from myself. I noticed a small hole in the middle of me some months back. Recently it has grown larger and larger. I am afraid that if I stay here without touching my own land that I will disappear completely. I will no longer be Yvonne. Then I will have to change my name. I am already beginning to wonder who I am. I am certain that the mountain knows exactly who she is.

It is around this time that another man comes into my life. And leaves as quickly as he comes. There is nothing much to him. His body is thin and light, which is exactly what I feel I need. His face is smooth and his lips are soft. The first time he bathes my face with kisses I forget the mountain completely. When he presses down against me I forget that selfish old man and his shiny head and false teeth. This man makes my body glow, and even though his eyes seem fake, even though when he looks at me they seem to be sucking me up, there is something in his laughter that makes him real. And he has a tongue that makes my body scream and chuckle with delight. For a moment I have a total break from the mountain. Somehow the terrible crashing sound of the volcano that used to explode in my head disappears, and when he caresses me, all the sounds and images of that dreadful volcano vanish and the terrible feeling of burning and choking is gone. He comes to me in the dead of night bringing his sweet music. It sounds like D'Angelo.

I believe it must be the smell of sulphur that I carry in my mouth that makes him stop coming. He says that he needs to commit more time to work, but I don't believe him, because even through those fake eyes I know he desires me. When it ends I have terrible nightmares. The flames are once again rolling down the hills. A deep black mud is covering up all my life's bricks. All my lavender dreams are on fire. I am more bereft than ever. The loss of him is so great that one day, while listening to D'Angelo, I actually hear my heart splintering. When I look at him I suddenly see a vampire in collusion with the mountain. I am shocked and angry with myself for allowing this to happen. When I see him months later he is pale and wan. He looks drained, as dry as hay and I am not surprised. He has obviously been keeping company with other vampires. He is not my destiny after all. Seeing him like that I realize that only I can put this mountain behind me. No-one else.

The smell of sulphur rises through the earth.
This is the beginning of the end,
the dying of an old time
when we flee across the seas
in boats of foreign tongues,
and only our green sick can
cover the smell of sulphur.

Antigua with all its wild birds
for some will be the sanctuary.
St. Kitts' cane will energise
a few lone souls,

as our soles tramp these islands
looking for a saviour
who cannot be resurrected,
for resurrection comes but once.
When the volcano coughs up her belly
she will cover the Windwards too.
Like a terrorist she has no limits.

Then
then
then
the suitcases teeming
with odds and ends
telling a confused story
an assortment of bric-a-brac askew.
Georgetown
Charlestown
Bridgetown
and London town.
There is no Plymouth.
It is all the same,
even without endless
black beaches
and saw-toothed mountains,
it is all the same.

One lone woman,
her thin skirt blowing in the breeze,
begins to dream again.
But there is no knight in shining armour
riding on a white horse.
Only a bus passes by,

overful with young men whose hungry eyes
claim this foreign woman.
She must be looking for a man,
she alone
she from Montserrat
she going need help, Jack.
They see all her needs
through her thin skirt
but they will offer
no more than a limp penile gesture
which she laughs at.

She has seen flames roll
down dark hills at night
and black mud has covered
all her hopes and dreams.
And then
then
then
she carries the smell
of sulphur
in her mouth
like a gift.
These men will pass.
She
can
do all things
she
can.
She has faced
a mountain.

In Montserrat I was surrounded by an abundance of love. I miss all of my friends. I realize that they are like the bricks and mortar to me. I miss Patsy's sweet apple pie and her to-die-for coconut pie. I miss George Street teeming with life and those Fridays sitting on Patsy's steps listening to the sound of cool reggae music and the smell of ganja wafting from some place down the street, where our sons play basketball. I miss liming with John every Friday afternoon and having a ting and goat water at Harbour Court. I miss sitting on my grandmother's steps every Saturday, even though I don't seem to be able to make her really love me, and have to listen to her moan about everything under God's sun including Dada, my Mum, Aunty Ethel, Laureen, Tan Tan – the list goes on. But I miss all my grandmother's stories. I miss those long telephone conversations that I used to have about beauty, about life, love and laughter with John (2). Boy, I really learnt a lot from him. I miss having my cousin Laureen do my hair. I haven't met a single hairdresser since who has done my hair the way she did. I come out of hairdressers and nobody ever turns their heads. I miss her salon bustling with activity. I miss Kinky's wicked and naughty sense of humour. I miss Cepekee's mad jokes and Accident's calypsos. I miss Wilson's delicious fried chicken at lunchtime. I miss the family spirit of the Rainbow Theatre. And Myrle. And Kevin. Then there was Joe who always came to rehearsals with his shoes in his hands. And where is Doris who refused to perform without her shoes? And Big Soup who always took forever to get the lights together but who never failed us? I miss the sight of Cutter leading my son's school steelband, and my son standing like a real professional, like a man, playing the tenor pan. I miss the Evergreen Tree that even hurricane Hugo couldn't destroy. And I miss having God in my life. And I miss the infectious laughter of Audith. I miss Melvy's cool calm voice. I miss Gwen's beautiful stillness. I miss the wonderful warmth at work, which needs to be exported to this country.

And I feel guilty because I haven't been very good at staying in touch. I realize I need to do that. I think about this little England with its ridiculous statue of Nelson not able to make up its mind which way to turn, and the brown dryness of this island makes me pine even more for the Evergreen Tree. Bottled or canned, Montserrat could make a lot of money. There is a desperate shortage of warmth here. But then I remember the passion of that poet and wonder if our paths will ever cross again.

I think of all the wonderful work I did in culture, now covered by the mountain's venom. I think of all the wonderfully committed and talented people who ensured that it all happened. And I die. The mountain has killed me. I have begun to go to sleep at night and wake up every morning with such an overwhelming loneliness that even if you rocked my whole body it wouldn't make a difference. My loneliness has begun to roam in front of me wherever I go. I have to go home. I spend a whole Sunday crying. I hide because I dare not let my son see those tears. It is the first Sunday in December. I am not looking forward to Christmas. Almost every Montserratian I know is going home. My cousin Laureen calls me. She must have heard me crying. Of all the people in my family, I consider her to be the most sturdy. She is like a rock. She tells me she is heartbroken when she thinks about Montserrat. I spend the whole Sunday crying. Where is the Evergreen Tree? What has become of it? That night I barely sleep. The next morning I get up and pray that God will forgive me the bitterness I feel. I arrive at the LIAT office bright and early with my return tickets from last year and discover to my joy that they are still valid. So I'm going home. I have no idea where I'm going to get the money from to come back, but go I must. I sleep deeply that night. A tremendous burden has been lifted off my shoulders. I am going home. Montserrat is the tree. I am a leaf. Removed and plucked from the Evergreen Tree, I could wither and die.

CHAPTER 7

Rising from the Ashes

I do go home for Christmas 1997. The first song I hear playing is George Benson's "*Everything must change; nothing stays the same; everyone must change; no-one stays the same. The young become the old; and mysteries do unfold; for that's the way of life; no-one and nothing goes unchanged. There are not many things in life we can be sure of. Except rain comes from the clouds and sun lights up the skies and humming birds do fly.*"

I get over the Montserrat blues, one time. I get over it. I get over the mountain. Somewhere between the crossing on the ferry from Antigua, which makes me real sick, and going to church on Christmas Sunday morning, I realize that the mountain has taught me that there is nothing greater than the challenge of battling with life. I see a huge pile of garbage burning at the end of the pier. I also see the sunrise. I see those small wooden houses, stark and barren with no trees. I also see the deep blue ocean. I visit some old people in these new boxes, where they can't even plant a flower. I listen to their own stories of the mountain. Like them I acknowledge that I have walked through storms and come out with the sun above my head. For the first time ever, I see an open sewer, its reddish-brown muddy contents swirling around at the end of the street. I realize there is an ash of death and ash of rebirth. The hospital is filthy and unsightly, and since it was designed to be a school, it is clearly not designed to make people well. It reminds me of a broken-down shantytown. But I look up to God above who has blown the creative muse into my face. From a small hill, Nathan and I watch the runway of the airport. That's all that's left. There is an iron gate at Salem preventing me from getting through to the town. So I cannot see the Evergreen Tree, anyway. But I feel the ancestral spirits whisper to me.

Destruction and creation: that is all. A friend shows me a video of the entire South burnt to the ground, which it does on Boxing Day. The mountain has been busy even during the festive season. I am reminded that God created the heavens and the earth. I hear grown men say how much they miss their wives and families. I hear these men admit that they actually cry at the sight of their children leaving the island. I see them drink themselves silly on New Year's Day, when they think about their houses burning to the ground. I hear the voices of four thousand people determined to ride out the storm. And although there is no Mama to sit on the steps with any more, I can still feel her presence.

Her legs too arthritic
would not allow her to stand
yet she stood majestic as the pyramids.

Her eyes too dark
refused to recognize familiar faces
yet she knew the beauty of every flower in her garden.

Her skin too leathery and worn
to be touched by hands of love
yet she recalled her lover's fingers soft across her face.

Her constant prayers too soft
to disturb her closest neighbours
deafened her God who, hearing them,
lifted them up high.

And I get over the Montserrat blues. For I am complete.

I remember Mama saying that God does not give us more than we can bear. She told me once that when the volcano goes back to sleep, the land is going be fertile and rich and we'll be able to plant even more food than before. The ash will produce sweet potatoes that will be sweeter, and dasheens will be bigger, and the yams will have more nourishment. So I know I must not give up. Victory will be mine. I can do all things I can. I need to plant an evergreen tree in my heart and call it Montserrat. No matter how powerful the mountain is, she cannot destroy what I plant in my heart. I can water it with tears of love and joy, or I can water it with tears of bitterness and anguish. I can nourish it with hope and optimism, or I can poison it with despair and depression. I can allow it to sustain me or I can allow it to oppress me. I can either brood over my loss, or build a new Montserrat, a Montserrat full of my Mama's stories, with my son shining behind me. I know, even without seeing her, that the Evergreen tree still stands. I will rise out of the ashes. This testimony is my own affirmation. Is my rebirth out of those ashes. I know which path I will take. I have faced a mountain. When the mountain roared at me, I roared right back. Perhaps there is a brilliant sun ahead.

Soufriere. The mountain. The living volcano. The now-awakened giant. Eight years later she still rages. But there is still a brilliant sun ahead. This is the beginning of a new time.

OTHER TITLES FROM MONTSERRAT

Howard Fergus
Lara Rains & Colonial Rites
ISBN: 0-948833-95-5, pub. 1998, pp.88, Price: £6.95

Howard Fergus's poems explore the nature of living on Montserrat, a 'two-be-three island/hard like rock', vulnerable to the forces of nature (Hurricane Hugo and the erupting Soufriere) and still 'this British corridor'. He writes honestly and observantly about these contingencies, finding in them metaphors for experiences which are universal. Nature's force strips life to its essentials ('Soufriere opened a new bible/in her pulpit in the hills/ to teach us the arithmetic of days') and reveals creation and destruction as one ('We celebrate Hugo child of God/ he killed and made alive for a season').

In a small island society, individual lives take on an enhanced significance: they are its one true resource and the sequence of obituary poems brings home with force how irreplaceable they are. Beyond Montserrat, Fergus looks for a wider Caribbean unity, but finds it only in cricket (and crime). Cricket, indeed, provides a major focus for his sense of the ironies of Caribbean history: that through a white-flannelled colonial rite with its roots in an imperial sense of Englishness, the West Indies has found its only true political framework and the means, explored in the sequence of poems celebrating Brian Lara's feats of 1994, to overturn symbolically the centuries of enslavement and colonialism.

Stewart Brown writes in the *Longman Caribbean New Voices 1*, 'Fergus is a poet of real stature'.

Howard Fergus
Volcano Verses
ISBN: 1-900715-79-1, pub. 2003, pp. 84, price £7.99

Howard Fergus is amongst a very small minority of Montserratians. He lives in Montserrat. Emigration has taken generations away and the 1997 eruption of Soufrière destroyed two-thirds of its habitable space, its economy and drove the majority of its inhabitants into exile. The poems in *Volcano Verses* express the confidence that island life and folk will outlast volcanic tantrums, that though 'Tonight Chances pique still grows/...But cattle low and egrets ride/ Inspite of fire from mountain tides'.

What Fergus is doing in the book is writing against the absences, writing into being again the people who have gone, the landscape utterly transformed, the society fragmented. The eruption has instigated the sternest truth-telling, the sense of a world purified, but it has also prompted a hugely heightened consciousness of the importance of the seemingly trivial, the myriad social interactions, the sounds, the smells of a literally vanished world. It is the very absences, the restriction of current possibility that drives Fergus to greater abundance of creation, in the conversational, muscular rhythms, the serious word-play that characterise his most mature and distinctive collection yet.

E.A. Markham
Marking Time
ISBN: 1-900715-29-5, pub. 1999, pp. 262, £7.99

Pewter Stapleton is drowning under a pile of marking. He teaches creative writing at a university in Sheffield, a campus peopled with malign cost-cutting accountants, baffled security staff and colleagues cloning themselves.

Pewter is a brilliant comic creation, an endless lister of tasks which are never quite completed, who is strung forever between seriousness and send-up, a commitment to his writing and boundless cynicism about writers and the arts industry.

From Pewter's desk and his marking, the novel radiates backwards and forwards in time, to his childhood in the small volcanic Caribbean island of St. Caesare (a version of Montserrat) and memories of his headmaster, the libidinous Professeur Croissant and Horace his half-mad cousin, and to his relationships with Carrington, a highly successful Caribbean writer whose plays Pewter is editing, to Balham, a professional of the race industry (where Pewter is a self-admitted slow learner in blackness) and to Lee, the woman he loves, but who despairs of him as 'sporadic'.

As a novel about life and writing, factuality and invention rub shoulders to hilarious effect as Pewter is incessantly driven to turn his experiences, his friends and their experiences into works of drama and fiction.

Jim Hannan writes in *World Literature Today*: 'Markham demonstrates a laudable range of talents, and shows himself to possess an inquisitive, keenly perceptive, and jocular mind. *Marking Time* succeeds in part because of its broad perspective not only on Caribbean affairs but on contemporary English manners and society. Readers of this book will undoubtedly hope that Markham will publish another novel soon.'

E.A. Markham
Taking the Drawing Room Through Customs:
Selected Stories 1972-2002
ISBN: 1-900715-69-4, pub. 2002, pp. 332, price £9.99

When E.A. Markham writes a story about the Other World Cup (Montserrat loses 4-0 to Bhutan – the volcanic eruption has destroyed all the football pitches in Montserrat) and a few months later is actually invited to a literature festival in Bhutan, this chimes in with his fiction. In 1972, his alter ego, Pewter Stapleton, invented the island of St Caesare (next door to Montserrat, but more independent-minded) as part of an elaborate scam to enjoy the rich perks of a UN conference. Since then, the island has been pencilled in on a couple of maps; and a handful of people claim to have been there.

Conventional narrative could never convey the complexities of the recurrent and entertaining cast of mainly Caribbean characters as they make sense of their remembered and reinvented lives. Digression becomes an art form both in Pewter Stapleton's narration and in their stories. It is the rich web of words they weave that leads Markham to his image of the drawing room as a repository of the talk of family and friends as perhaps the most valuable possession taken by Caribbean people through Customs.

Boyd Tonkin writes in *The Independent*:
'Markham's deadpan wit and self-protective irony never desert him. He's never less than funny, and never less than moving. The English-speaking Caribbean has bred some wonderful wanderers from his generation, but none (certainly not Walcott or Naipaul) can boast a literary voice as wryly companionable as this.'

Go to www.peepaltreepress.com to find full details of almost three hundred titles in print – the very best of Caribbean and Black British writing.

All Peepal Tree books should be available through your local bookseller, though you are even more welcome to place orders direct with us on the Peepal Tree website and on-line bookstore. You can also order direct by phone or in writing.

Peepal Tree sends out regular e-mail information about new books and special offers. We also produce a twice-yearly stock catalogue, and new and forthcoming titles catalalogue to keep you up to date with what's coming up. Contact us to join our mailing list.

You can contact Peepal Tree at:

    17 King's Avenue
    Leeds LS6 1QS
    United Kingdom

    e-mail contact@peepaltreepress.com
    tel: 44 (0)113 245 1703
    website: www.peepaltreepress.com